Prayers AND Promises FOR Healing

JOAN HUNTER

BroadStreet
PUBLISHING

BroadStreet Publishing Group, LLC
Racine, Wisconsin, USA
BroadStreetPublishing.com

Prayers AND *Promises* FOR *Healing*

IMPORTANT: This book is a resource for encouragement, hope, and prayer because we believe that Jesus Christ has paid the price for our healing. The author and publisher do not claim to treat or diagnose any disease or illness and are not responsible for anyone's healing. The information in this book is not a substitute for professional advice or medical treatment.

Printed in China
17 18 19 20 5 4 3 2

Contents

INTRODUCTION

I've had the privilege of being involved in the ministry of healing for over forty-five years. During that time I've observed that many problems that manifest in the soul or body have a spiritual root. When we consider the root of any condition, then we can address that area specifically and not just treat the symptom with medicine and hope it goes away. I encourage you to seek the advice of professionals, and I also encourage you to use this book's prayers and promises as you seek the miracle you need right now.

This book is arranged by topics that describe a condition you do not want to have (addiction, fear, sickness) or something you do want to have (freedom, hope, wisdom). Each contains a short introduction to provide insight about that topic, related Scriptures from God's Word, and a prayer of faith to declare. Your words are powerful! Use them to bless, strengthen your faith, and start a conversation with God that goes much deeper than what is contained in these pages.

It's my hope and prayer that this resource helps you to stand on the promises of God for your own life and on behalf of those you love. May this book be a great encouragement to you in your quest for the healing that God has provided in Jesus Christ. You can be healed, set free, and made completely whole—body, mind, and spirit!

Joan Hunter

As society has rejected moral foundations, people have become increasingly callous in stealing, gossiping, lying, and hurting others. Selfishness and entitlement have driven human behavior to new levels of violence. Sexual, physical, emotional, and mental abuse abound in our culture.

Unfortunately, some have responded to their sufferings by adopting the identity of a victim. They have become accustomed to receiving attention, care, and money because of their pain, disabilities, and troubles, and they don't want to give it all up in order to be healed.

No matter how devastating the abuse experienced, in order to be whole we must earnestly seek the Great Physician without clinging to the identity of being a victim. Jesus who was crucified for us is also the one who will heal us.

He was broken for your healing. His blood was poured out for your cleansing from all pain and suffering. He is able to make you completely whole and remove the wounds and scars of the past. God loves you and He will care for you.

PROMISES

The LORD is near to the brokenhearted
and saves the crushed in spirit.
> PSALM 34:18 ESV

LORD, you know the hopes of the helpless.
Surely you will hear their cries and comfort them.
You will bring justice to the orphans
  and the oppressed,
so mere people can no longer terrify them.
> PSALM 10:17–18 NLT

The LORD hears his people
  when they call to him for help.
He rescues them from all their troubles.
> PSALM 34:17 NLT

But you, God, see the trouble of the afflicted;
you consider their grief and take it in hand.
The victims commit themselves to you;
you are the helper of the fatherless.
> PSALM 10:14 NIV

So we do not lose heart. Though our outer self is
wasting away, our inner self is being renewed day
by day.
> 2 CORINTHIANS 4:16 ESV

But You, O LORD, are a shield about me,
My glory, and the One who lifts my head.

PSALM 3:3 NASB

PRAYER

Jesus, I know you hear my cries. Take me to a safe place where I can be free from the abuse I have experienced. I refuse every lie I have believed about myself and the abuse of my past. Holy Spirit, guide me into all truth.

Father, I forgive those who have hurt me and ask you to make things right. Heal the painful memories and make me whole.

Thank you, Lord Jesus, for loving me. Come and heal all my wounds and release me from every sorrow. I trust you to take all my pain and replace it with your joy. Take my brokenness and make me whole. Heal my heart and release me from all the abuse I have suffered, and fill me with your peace.

God, you are a shield all around me. You are renewing my inner self each day, and you will rescue me from all my troubles. I declare that I am not a victim. I am a victor and overcomer in Jesus' name! Amen.

Being controlled by anything or anyone other than God can be destructive to our body, soul, and spirit. Addictive behaviors can form in any number of ways, but what is most important to understand is that they come from the enemy. Satan offers us an enticing open door to fall into evil and miss God's purpose for our lives. Since Satan was kicked out of heaven, his vendetta against God is to destroy what God loves, namely, His children.

Being hooked or seriously controlled by anything or anyone other than God distorts our free will and choices. Our addictions only separate us from God.

The word *addiction* is often attached to drugs or alcohol, but people can also be addicted to pornography, cigarettes, food, television, shopping, and much more. If you are stuck in the midst of addiction, don't be discouraged because you can be free from your addictive behavior.

God's deliverance is the only way to bring total healing and freedom from the control of evil spirits tied to these addictions. If you are addicted to something that is not good for you, know and trust that Jesus Christ can set you free to experience peace and freedom in Him.

Promises

No temptation has overtaken you except what is common to mankind. And God is faithful; he will not let you be tempted beyond what you can bear. But when you are tempted, he will also provide a way out so that you can endure it.
> 1 Corinthians 10:13 niv

This means that anyone who belongs to Christ has become a new person. The old life is gone; a new life has begun!
> 2 Corinthians 5:17 nlt

So if the Son sets you free, you are truly free.
> John 8:36 nlt

Finally, brothers, whatever is true, whatever is honorable, whatever is just, whatever is pure, whatever is lovely, whatever is commendable, if there is any excellence, if there is anything worthy of praise, think about these things.
> Philippians 4:8 esv

Prayer

Father, I want to be free from every form of addiction and control in my life. I want every desire to be toward you and the good things you have for me.

I confess to you my addiction to ___. Change my desires. I don't want to be bound any more. Forgive me for rebelling against you and your will for my life, and free me from every addictive behavior that has kept me enslaved to its will. I want nothing to blur a clear path to you, God.

For parts of me that have been damaged by my addictions, I ask that you would replace them now with new parts from heaven. Make me whole and wholly yours. If I need peace, I will come to you. If I need safety, I will come to you.

I praise you, Father, for your saving grace and mercy. You are faithful and will not allow me to be tempted beyond what I can handle with your help. I set my mind on all that is good and will look for your way of escape whenever I am tempted. I am a new creation in Christ. The old is gone; a new life has begun, in Jesus' name, amen.

Anger

A challenge we all face is learning how to relate to people and events that don't meet our expectations. When our expectations are not met, many of us respond in anger. Unchecked anger can cause a person to react in unhealthy ways. Decisions made or actions taken while angry usually lead to greater problems and more frustration in the future.

Everyone has to learn to put these matters in God's hands and allow Him to bring about a good result in His own time. Releasing the disappointment to God allows you to maintain a clear head and protects you and others from making foolish decisions.

The Bible has much to say about anger—not only about anger itself, but also about how we are not to respond in anger. Some anger is righteous, but other anger is unhealthy and unholy. God wants us to see things from His perspective and respond with His heart. Instead of anger, let's ask God to give us patience and kindness.

When life doesn't go as planned, instead of getting angry, see these as opportunities for God break through in your situation and to transform you and strengthen you, causing you to grow in faith, exhibit the character of Christ more fully, and see God break through on your behalf.

Promises

My dear brothers and sisters, take note of this: Everyone should be quick to listen, slow to speak and slow to become angry, because human anger does not produce the righteousness that God desires.

JAMES 1:19–20 NIV

Whoever is slow to anger has great understanding, but he who has a hasty temper exalts folly.

PROVERBS 14:29 ESV

Do not be overcome by evil, but overcome evil with good.

ROMANS 12:21 ESV

A fool vents all his feelings,
But a wise man holds them back.

PROVERBS 29:11 NKJV

"In your anger do not sin": Do not let the sun go down while you are still angry, and do not give the devil a foothold.

EPHESIANS 4:26–27 NIV

Sensible people control their temper;
they earn respect by overlooking wrongs.

PROVERBS 19:11 NLT

Beloved, do not avenge yourselves, but rather give place to wrath; for it is written, "Vengeance is Mine, I will repay," says the Lord.

ROMANS 12:19 NKJV

PRAYER

Father God, I give you all my disappointments and things that did not go my way. Heal my heart and make it whole. I repent for my angry reactions to people and events that did not meet my expectations. I lay down all my unmet expectations of ___ to you and I ask you to love people through me regardless of their actions or words.

Fill me with your love and remove all selfish ambition and self-centeredness from me. I leave all the things that trouble me in your hands, and I refuse to give into anger.

Lord, I give you my anger and trust you to make things right. I will not vent all my feelings and will be a person who is slow to anger. Even when I am angry, I will not sin, but will overcome all evil with good, in Jesus' name, amen!

Assurance

God is our Father and He does not change. The Bible tells us that God can do all things, and it also tells us that He is incapable of lying. This means that the Lord is always faithful and true. Whatever He says, He will perform and bring it about in His time.

Every word He speaks to you can be trusted—100 percent of the time. He is invincible, unstoppable, and utterly relentless. He is your eternal rock and exceedingly great reward. He will finish what He has started in your life.

We will experience circumstances in life where we will doubt, and we will seem to lose faith. But in that place—in the midst of hopelessness and the lack of assurance—God reassures us of His nature, of His great love for us, and of His provision on our behalf.

Place your hand in His and hang on today. Place your family, your work, and your life at His feet and watch what He will do. Be assured, for placing your faith in God is the best decision you will ever make.

Promises

His divine power has granted to us all things that pertain to life and godliness, through the knowledge of him who called us to his own glory and excellence, by which he has granted to us his precious and very great promises, so that through them you may become partakers of the divine nature, having escaped from the corruption that is in the world because of sinful desire.

2 Peter 1:3–4 esv

Jesus Christ is the same yesterday and today and forever.

Hebrews 13:8 nasb

Now to him who is able to do immeasurably more than all we ask or imagine, according to his power that is at work within us, to him be glory in the church and in Christ Jesus throughout all generations, for ever and ever! Amen.

Ephesians 3:20–21 niv

I have set the Lord always before me;
because he is at my right hand, I shall not be shaken.
Therefore my heart is glad,
    and my whole being rejoices;
my flesh also dwells secure.
For you will not abandon my soul to Sheol,

or let your holy one see corruption.
You make known to me the path of life;
in your presence there is fullness of joy;
at your right hand are pleasures forevermore.

PSALM 16:8–11 ESV

Dear friends, if we don't feel guilty, we can come to
God with bold confidence.

1 JOHN 3:21 NLT

PRAYER

Father God, thank you for your many promises to me
and for your reassurance in the midst of my doubt and
unbelief. I thank you that your promises to me are true
and they cannot fail. Your thoughts toward me are too
numerous to count, and they are always kind. Because
you are always the same, I trust that I will find all I need
in you, Jesus. Your words are my daily bread and I am
fully assured in you.

You are able to do above all that I could ever ask or
imagine. You are near to me and I will not be shaken.
Through your great promises I will partake of our divine
nature, escaping the corruption of this world, and be all
that you've created me to be in Jesus.

Thank you that I can come to you with full assurance today because of Jesus' finished work on the
cross. Amen.

Belief

Sometimes it seems as if we struggle with our belief in the promises that God has given to us. We know He promised to heal us, but we find ourselves sick. Maybe He promised to give you freedom, but you are struggling with addictions and vices. No matter what our outward circumstances look like today, God tells us to keep on believing in Him, trusting that what He has promised will surely come to pass.

Everything in the kingdom of God hinges on faith and belief in God. It is the pivot point upon which all the riches of God turn and manifest for those who look to Him. Faith moves mountains, extinguishes fires, multiplies provision, raises the dead, heals the sick, casts out demons, closes the mouths of lions, creates paths through dark waters, gives birth through barren wombs, and above all else, it pleases God. He loves faith, and those who choose to believe can see Him work wonders.

Promises

And without faith it is impossible to please him, for whoever would draw near to God must believe that he exists and that he rewards those who seek him.

HEBREWS 11:6

If you declare with your mouth, "Jesus is Lord," and believe in your heart that God raised him from the dead, you will be saved. For it is with your heart that you believe and are justified, and it is with your mouth that you profess your faith and are saved.

ROMANS 10:9–10 NIV

"What do you mean, 'If I can'?" Jesus asked. "Anything is possible if a person believes."

MARK 9:23 NLT

So they said, "Believe on the Lord Jesus Christ, and you will be saved, you and your household."

ACTS 16:31 NKJV

Jesus told her, "I am the one who raises the dead and gives them life again. Anyone who believes in me, even though he dies like anyone else, shall live again."

JOHN 11:25 TLB

"Have faith in God," Jesus answered. "Truly I tell you, if anyone says to this mountain, 'Go, throw yourself into the sea,' and does not doubt in their heart but believes that what they say will happen, it will be done for them. Therefore I tell you, whatever you ask for in prayer, believe that you have received it, and it will be yours."

MARK 11:22–24 NIV

Prayer

God, heal every area of my heart that has been hurt by life's circumstances and tells me to doubt your goodness and grace in my life. I want to trust you with everything in my being. I live by faith in you, Lord.

Every part of me rejoices in you and relies on you, even though I'm waiting for your promise to come to pass. You promised that all things are possible to those who believe. Lord, I believe and I trust that you are faithful and able to bring breakthrough in my life.

Give me the faith that moves mountains, the belief that trusts you despite what I see with my eyes. I will declare with my mouth the promises in your Word.

You are a rewarder of those who seek you, and I want you to be a part of every area in my life, Lord. I say to the mountains in my life: move! I can do all things through Christ who gives me strength. Amen!

Children

Children are a blessing from God, a precious gift given by Him. They are a heritage to carry on the family name, and a blessing to the future. Children are to be the embodiment of love produced by an act of love between a man and a woman. To guide a child on the path to eternal life with God is an honor and a great responsibility.

Children bring great joy and blessing into a family; however, they can also bring strife and great challenges. Sometimes parents wonder if their children will ever learn obedience or safely survive tough years while growing up.

To raise a child in the way God has for him or her requires prayer and daily wisdom from God's Word. No matter how difficult or busy life gets in raising your children, remember that they are a blessing from God, a gift of God's grace to this world.

PROMISES

Direct your children onto the right path,
and when they are older, they will not leave it.
PROVERBS 22:6 NLT

And anyone who welcomes a little child like this on my behalf is welcoming me. Beware that you don't look down on any of these little ones. For I tell you that in heaven their angels are always in the presence of my heavenly Father.

MATTHEW 18:5, 10 NLT

Children are a gift from the LORD;
they are a reward from him.

PSALM 127:3 NLT

I have no greater joy than to hear that my children are walking in the truth.

3 JOHN 4 NIV

See how very much our Father loves us, for he calls us his children, and that is what we are! But the people who belong to this world don't recognize that we are God's children because they don't know him. Dear friends, we are already God's children, but he has not yet shown us what we will be like when Christ appears. But we do know that we will be like him, for we will see him as he really is.

1 JOHN 3:1–2 NLT

So they said, "Believe on the Lord Jesus Christ, and you will be saved, you and your household."

ACTS 16:31 NKJV

But if serving the LORD seems undesirable to you, then choose for yourselves this day whom you will serve, whether the gods your ancestors served beyond the Euphrates, or the gods of the Amorites, in whose land you are living. But as for me and my household, we will serve the LORD.

JOSHUA 24:15 NIV

PRAYER

Father, thank you for children—gifts and blessings of new life. My child is a reward that has come from you. Heal any brokenness in our relationship. Help us to forgive each other. I invite you to come and restore all that has been lost.

Give me the wisdom I need every day to encourage and direct my child onto your paths of righteousness. Remind me to talk about your ways whenever I'm with my child—when we're at home or away from home, when we're going to bed and when we wake up.

I declare that each child is a gift that comes from your loving and gracious hands. Thank you that every one of them will be saved, walk in your light and truth, and be with you for eternity. As for me and my house, we will serve the Lord. Amen!

Comfort

We all face sickness, grief, loss, and death at some point in our lives. It is in those times where we need to experience a comfort that doesn't come from this world, but a comfort that can only come from God. No amount of earthly comfort can soothe a weary soul like the comfort that comes from God. Only He can provide the deep peace we need in the midst of our storm.

Jesus called the Holy Spirit our Comforter. The Holy Spirit is the one who encircles the children of God to console them as they journey through a broken world. The Triune God watches over His own, to care for them and to perform His will through them.

Receive God's comfort today, knowing that God will cause everything to work out for your best, even in those moments that are most difficult and painful. God is always near, and He will give you the comfort you need in the moment you need it. He is near to you, comforting you with His unfailing love.

Promises

May your unfailing love be my comfort,
according to your promise to your servant.
PSALM 119:76 NIV

Now may our Lord Jesus Christ himself and God
our Father, who loved us and by his grace gave us
eternal comfort and a wonderful hope, comfort you
and strengthen you in every good thing you do and
say.
2 THESSALONIANS 2:16–17 NLT

Unless the LORD had helped me,
I would soon have settled in the silence of the grave.
I cried out, "I am slipping!"
but your unfailing love, O LORD, supported me.
When doubts filled my mind,
your comfort gave me renewed hope and cheer.
PSALM 94:17–19 NLT

Blessed be the God and Father of our Lord Jesus
Christ, the Father of mercies and God of all comfort,
who comforts us in all our tribulation, that we may
be able to comfort those who are in any trouble,
with the comfort with which we ourselves are
comforted by God.
2 CORINTHIANS 1:3–4 NKJV

These things I have spoken to you while I am still with you. But the Helper, the Holy Spirit, whom the Father will send in my name, he will teach you all things and bring to your remembrance all that I have said to you. Peace I leave with you; my peace I give to you. Not as the world gives do I give to you. Let not your hearts be troubled, neither let them be afraid.

JOHN 14:25–27 ESV

PRAYER

Holy Spirit, you are my Comforter. Every moment of every day, you are all that I need. Fill me with your presence and peace. Heal my heart, my body, my soul, and my mind from all trauma and release your comfort into every area of my life. You will bring me through every difficult and painful circumstance. Not only will you bring me through them, you also will comfort me in the middle of them, giving me a peace that doesn't come from this world.

You are helping me and healing me. Give me an eternal comfort and a wonderful hope, and strengthen me in every good thing I do and say today. In the midst of my trouble, I cry out to you. Your unfailing love supports me and is my comfort. Amen.

Confidence

It's dangerous to put our confidence in earthly abilities, gifts, or achievements. Instead our confidence should be in Jesus Christ and Him alone. When we experience times of doubt, timidity, or insecurity, that's the time to lean most heavily on Christ. If everything was perfect in this world, we would have no need for confidence.

We do not need more self-confidence—confidence in *ourselves*. We need the rich confidence that only comes from trusting in and relying on God. This type of confidence will cause you to declare: "You are my God and I am not ashamed to be numbered with you no matter who hates you or what they say about me. Though others forsake you, I will hold firm in my confidence in you. Though a thousand fall at my side and ten thousand at my right hand, still I will trust you."

Promises

So we can confidently say,
"The Lord is my helper;
I will not fear;
what can man do to me?"
HEBREWS 13:6 ESV

Let us then approach God's throne of grace with confidence, so that we may receive mercy and find grace to help us in our time of need.
HEBREWS 4:16 NIV

But blessed is the man who trusts in the Lord and has made the Lord his hope and confidence.
JEREMIAH 17:7 TLB

God gives them confidence and strength, and helps them in many ways.
JOB 24:23 TLB

And this is the confidence that we have toward him, that if we ask anything according to his will he hears us. And if we know that he hears us in whatever we ask, we know that we have the requests that we have asked of him.
1 JOHN 5:14–15 ESV

For I am confident of this very thing, that He who began a good work in you will perfect it until the day of Christ Jesus.

PHILIPPIANS 1:6 NASB

PRAYER

God, you are my ever-present help in my time of need. Because you are my helper, I will not fear what others can do to me. You are the one who gives me confidence and strength, and you help me in so many ways.

God, I come boldly to your throne today to find grace and mercy in my time of need. I thank you that my confidence in is in you, and you cannot be moved. I put my trust in you today, for I have made you my hope and my confidence.

Heal wounds in my heart that produce insecurity, timidity, uncertainty, and other things that tempt me to doubt your goodness and power in my life to do all that you've called me to do. You hear every word I pray to you. Because you are my helper and my strength, and I will not fear. Amen!

Courage

Followers of Jesus Christ must be able to face difficult challenges and know that God will give them victory over the giants in the land, remove that mountain that stands in front of them, still that storm, multiply that food, close the mouths of lions, deliver them from a flood, interpret that dream, quench that fire, guide them through darkness and deep waters, take them out of prison, give them words to say to their enemies, defend them from adversaries, and protect them from principalities and powers. All we need to face these types of circumstances is godly courage.

As we follow Jesus, we will face opposition. Some will even attack us because of our allegiance to Jesus, but He is greater than them all. During times of persecution or isolation, He will never leave us or forsake us. In this world we may experience tribulation, but He has overcome the world.

Jesus is the victor. He is the one who makes you brave, giving you the ability and audacity to stand up in the midst of the storm. God is the one who gives you courage to face whatever this life may bring.

Promises

You need only to be strong and courageous and to obey to the letter every law Moses gave you, for if you are careful to obey every one of them, you will be successful in everything you do.

JOSHUA 1:7 TLB

Have I not commanded you? Be strong and courageous. Do not be frightened, and do not be dismayed, for the LORD your God is with you wherever you go.

JOSHUA 1:9 ESV

Even though I walk through the valley
of the shadow of death,
I fear no evil, for You are with me;
Your rod and Your staff, they comfort me.

PSALM 23:4 NASB

When I am afraid, I put my trust in you.
In God, whose word I praise—
in God I trust and am not afraid.
What can mere mortals do to me?

PSALM 56:3–4 NIV

Finally, be strong in the Lord and in his mighty power. Put on the full armor of God, so that you can take your stand against the devil's schemes.

EPHESIANS 6:10–11 NIV

Love the LORD, all you godly ones!
For the LORD protects those who are loyal to him,
but he harshly punishes the arrogant.
So be strong and courageous,
all you who put your hope in the LORD!

PSALM 31:23–24 NLT

So do not throw away this confident trust in the Lord. Remember the great reward it brings you! Patient endurance is what you need now, so that you will continue to do God's will. Then you will receive all that he has promised.

HEBREWS 10:35–36 NLT

PRAYER

When I am afraid, God, I will put my trust in you, for you are my helper and the one who gives me courage. I will be strong and courageous today, obeying everything you have told me to do. I will not be frightened or dismayed, because you, Lord, are with me wherever I go. With you by my side, I have courage to face the valley of the shadow of death.

So I choose to be strong in the Lord and in the power of His might today, trusting that you will give me the courage I need to face giants in my life. Confident trust in the Lord brings great reward! I put all my hope in you, Jesus. Amen.

Deliverance

God is our deliverer. Whatever it is we may need deliverance from, He is the only one who can break its power and set us free to live a godly life in Christ Jesus. Whether we need deliverance from mental illness, demonic activity, or addictions; or if we need deliverance from a physical ailment, such as cancer or a common cold; or from an enemy who seems to be assaulting us; Jesus Christ is the one we look to and the one we call out to for that deliverance.

Who will deliver us from evil? God is our deliverer, plucking us out of the fires of affliction and delivering us from the power of sin. He delivers us from the attacks of the enemy, both spiritual and natural. We overcome darkness as we cling to Him, and all evil flees from His presence. He triumphed over death and the grave by the cross of Jesus Christ. He took the keys of death and hell from Satan and ascended to the right hand of God. That is why we call Him Savior and Lord.

Whatever you may need today, know that He is the God who brings deliverance to His people.

Promises

The LORD hears his people when
  they call to him for help.
He rescues them from all their troubles.
> PSALM 34:17 NLT

But as for me, my prayer is to you, O LORD.
At an acceptable time, O God,
in the abundance of your steadfast love answer me
in your saving faithfulness.
Deliver me from sinking in the mire;
let me be delivered from my enemies
and from the deep waters....
Answer me, O LORD, for your steadfast love is good;
according to your abundant mercy, turn to me.
> PSALM 69:13–14, 16 ESV

The righteous person faces many troubles,
but the LORD comes to the rescue each time.
> PSALM 34:19 NLT

You are my hiding place;
You preserve me from trouble;
You surround me with songs of deliverance.
> PSALM 32:7 NASB

God is to us a God of deliverances;
And to GOD the Lord belong escapes from death.
> PSALM 68:20 NASB

He has delivered us from the power of darkness and conveyed us into the kingdom of the Son of His love.

COLOSSIANS 1:13 NKJV

But the Lord is faithful, and he will strengthen you and protect you from the evil one.

2 THESSALONIANS 3:3 NIV

PRAYER

Father, I thank you that you have given me the ultimate deliverance—you have taken me out of the kingdom of darkness and placed me in the kingdom of the Son of your love. You are my deliverer.

God, you are my hiding place. Surround me with songs of deliverance. Thank you that you hear when I call for help, and that you come to the rescue each time.

Your love is steadfast and you are faithful! You will deliver me and protect me from the evil one. Thank you! To you belong all power and authority, and so I rejoice in you, my Savior and my Lord.

Depression

God created humans as spiritual beings and placed them in a garden where they had no disappointments to overcome. When Adam and Eve chose to disobey God and were enticed by the enemy to sin, their spirits were darkened and the glory of God's immediate, manifest presence departed. Where there was perfect harmony before, now there was discord; and where there was enjoyment and happiness before, now there was depression. Since then people have searched for something to fill that spiritual void, but anything less than Jesus will always disappoint and depress.

Life apart from the presence of God is incomplete, disappointing, and depressing. However, the kingdom of God is full of righteousness, peace, and joy. That is not to say that godly people don't get depressed or discouraged. Traumatic life events, changes in hormones, sleep deprivation, and other factors contribute to the feeling of depression. The Bible encourages us to put our hope in God in every situation, to rejoice in the Lord, and that God is the one who lifts up our head.

God wants to lift you up out of depression and free you so you experience the oil of gladness instead of mourning, and the garment of praise instead of a faint spirit. Jesus can heal you of depression as you continually look to Him.

Promises

The LORD hears his people when
  they call to him for help.
He rescues them from all their troubles.
> PSALM 34:17 NLT

He has delivered us from the power of darkness and
conveyed us into the kingdom of the Son of His love.
> COLOSSIANS 1:13 NKJV

Why, my soul, are you downcast?
Why so disturbed within me?
Put your hope in God,
for I will yet praise him,
my Savior and my God.
> PSALM 42:11 NIV

But you, O LORD, are a shield about me,
my glory, and the lifter of my head.
> PSALM 3:3 ESV

To grant to those who mourn in Zion—
  to give them a beautiful headdress instead of ashes,
the oil of gladness instead of mourning,
  the garment of praise instead of a faint spirit;
that they may be called oaks of righteousness,
  the planting of the Lord, that he may be glorified.
> ISAIAH 61:3 ESV

But you are a chosen people, a royal priesthood, a holy nation, God's special possession, that you may declare the praises of him who called you out of darkness into his wonderful light.

1 PETER 2:9 NIV

Rejoice in the Lord always; again I will say, rejoice.

PHILIPPIANS 4:4 ESV

For this reason I bow my knees before the Father … that He would grant you, according to the riches of His glory, to be strengthened with power through His Spirit in the inner man.

EPHESIANS 3:14–16 NASB

PRAYER

Father God, you have not called me to a life of depression, but to a life of peace and joy in the Holy Spirit. Forgive me for believing lies that do not represent your heart. I release the people and situations that are weighing me down into your loving care.

I command my body's systems and frequencies to be in harmony and balance, the way God created my body to function. Spirit of depression, go now, in Jesus' name. Holy Spirit, I welcome your gladness and praise.

Jesus loves me! My hope is in God and I rejoice in you. You have chosen me and you are taking me out of darkness into your wonderful light. Amen.

Disability

The needs we have are God's opportunity to reveal Himself in a greater way and act on our behalf. He delights in our faith. He loves our conscious dependency on Him and when we turn to Him in prayer. All our earthly weaknesses and disabilities are opportunities for Him to show His love and power on our behalf. It gives Him the perfect conditions under which to reveal Himself and transform us into the glorious image of His Son.

Truly, only God is fully able to help us in the midst of our disabilities. We are His children and we depend on Him alone. He cares for us and acts on our behalf. He doesn't forsake His own. The Bible promises that God will never forget the needy. In fact, He is close to those who are helpless, and He longs to come near to those who are of a broken heart.

No matter what disability you may be facing today—whether it is physical, mental, emotional, or spiritual—God's grace is enough for you, for His strength is made perfect in weakness.

Promises

But God will never forget the needy;
the hope of the afflicted will never perish.
> PSALM 9:18 NIV

A bruised reed he will not break,
and a faintly burning wick he will not quench;
he will faithfully bring forth justice.
> ISAIAH 42:3 ESV

He gives power to the faint,
and to him who has no might he increases strength.
> ISAIAH 40:29 ESV

Three times I pleaded with the Lord about this, that
it should leave me. But he said to me, "My grace
is sufficient for you, for my power is made perfect
in weakness." Therefore I will boast all the more
gladly of my weaknesses, so that the power of Christ
may rest upon me. For the sake of Christ, then, I
am content with weaknesses, insults, hardships,
persecutions, and calamities. For when I am weak,
then I am strong.
> 2 CORINTHIANS 12:8–10 ESV

PRAYER

Lord, I thank you that you are always able and willing to enable me to overcome my disabilities. Wrap your supernatural ability around my disability and do something amazing with my life.

You strengthen me when I am weak, and give me grace that is sufficient to meet any weakness I may have. Your grace is sufficient for every need I have.

Only you can make up the difference for my weakness. I trust you to give me power when I feel faint and increase my strength when I am weak. I ask that you would strengthen me in hope, and that you would be my constant companion and help in time of need. Thank you, Jesus. Amen.

Discouragement

Every day holds the opportunity to be discouraged. Whether something happens that is big or small, the feelings of discouragement can be overwhelming and lead us to a dark place. These are the moments when we need to look to the Lord and ask Him for guidance. In these times we must persevere, relying on Him while doing all we can encourage ourselves in the Lord.

When we seek the Lord in that place of discouragement, He will give us the needed tools to do what He has called us to do. We will then be able to pursue, overtake, and recover all that has been lost.

God has already declared your victory. Encourage yourself in the Lord, seek His will, and He will lead you into victory no matter the situation you may face.

PROMISES

So do not lose the courage you had in the past, which has a great reward. You must hold on, so you can do what God wants and receive what he has promised.

HEBREWS 10:35–36 NCV

We are pressed on every side by troubles, but we are not crushed. We are perplexed, but not driven to despair. We are hunted down, but never abandoned by God. We get knocked down, but we are not destroyed.

2 CORINTHIANS 4:8–9 NLT

What then shall we say to these things? If God is for us, who can be against us? He who did not spare his own Son but gave him up for us all, how will he not also with him graciously give us all things? Who shall bring any charge against God's elect? It is God who justifies. Who is to condemn? Christ Jesus is the one who died—more than that, who was raised—who is at the right hand of God, who indeed is interceding for us. Who shall separate us from the love of Christ? Shall tribulation, or distress, or persecution, or famine, or nakedness, or danger, or sword? As it is written,

"For your sake we are being killed all the day long; we are regarded as sheep to be slaughtered."

No, in all these things we are more than conquerors through him who loved us. For I am sure that neither death nor life, nor angels nor rulers, nor things present nor things to come, nor powers, nor height nor depth, nor anything else in all creation, will be able to separate us from the love of God in Christ Jesus our Lord.

ROMANS 8:31–39 ESV

Prayer

Father, I refuse to give up or give in to discouragement. I know victory is in your hand, God. Even though I am pressed in from every side, I will not be crushed; even though I am perplexed, I won't be driven to despair; and even though I get knocked down at times, I will never be destroyed or abandoned by you, Lord.

I will encourage myself in your loving kindness today. All who look to you will be radiant, for they shall not be ashamed. So I look to you today for hope, light, and life.

Thank you, Father, that nothing shall separate me from the love of God in Christ Jesus. I declare that discouragement must go in Jesus' name. I am holding onto you, Jesus, so I can do what you want and receive what you have promised.

Faith

Faith is the victory that we have in Christ. It is the living substance that God uses to build our lives, both in this world and in the age to come. Faith is the vehicle to fulfill of all our hopes and all His promises. It empowers love, renews hope, banishes despair, protects the weak, and instructs the mind, defending it from vain imaginations, as well as shielding the heart from fatal attractions. Faith finds a way where there is no way, igniting courage and sustaining long-term commitments.

The Bible says that without faith it is impossible to please God. This doesn't mean that we can never have doubts, or that we'll never experience fears or hopes unfulfilled, but it does mean that we are to draw close to the Lord in the time of our weakness. We are to ask God to give us faith, and we are to ask Him to strengthen the measure of faith He has already given to us, and we are to do everything in our power to feed what He has placed in our heart.

As you seek God and meditate on His Word, He will sustain you with the needed faith to do His will and to experience breakthrough in your life.

Promises

Now faith is confidence in what we hope for and assurance about what we do not see.

HEBREWS 11:1 NIV

He said to them, "Because of your little faith. For truly, I say to you, if you have faith like a grain of mustard seed, you will say to this mountain, 'Move from here to there,' and it will move, and nothing will be impossible for you."

MATTHEW 17:20 ESV

And Jesus said to the man, "Stand up and go. Your faith has healed you."

LUKE 17:19 NLT

Indeed, none who wait for you
shall be put to shame;
they shall be ashamed who are wantonly
treacherous.

PSALM 25:3 ESV

So then faith comes by hearing, and hearing by the word of God.

ROMANS 10:17 NKJV

Prayer

Father God, I put all my confidence and trust in you. You tell me that faith comes by hearing, and hearing by the Word of God; so help me to meditate on your Word day and night and cause my faith to grow.

Increase my faith, Lord, and strengthen the measure of faith you have already given to me. Let your faith empower my love, renew my hope, and banish my despair. I want to please you, Lord, in every area of my life by the expression of my faith. By faith I speak to mountains in my life and say, "Be gone in Jesus' name." Nothing is impossible with God! Amen.

Family

Everyone has an earthly father and an eternal Father who is in heaven. In an ideal world, every father would embody the character and actions of the heavenly Father. Likewise, every mother would perfectly reflect the love and nurture of God. Many parents fall far short of this, but God never fails in His fatherly care of His children.

He is the perfect Father. He nurtures us and lovingly gives us the nature of His Son as we seek Him with our whole hearts. He is the perfect Father and the perfect example, and He is the Father from whom every father on earth derives its name. Praise be to the God and Father who created us for Himself.

PROMISES

But if serving the LORD seems undesirable to you, then choose for yourselves this day whom you will serve, whether the gods your ancestors served beyond the Euphrates, or the gods of the Amorites, in whose land you are living. But as for me and my household, we will serve the LORD.

JOSHUA 24:15 NIV

So they said, "Believe on the Lord Jesus Christ, and you will be saved, you and your household."

ACTS 16:31 NKJV

I am reminded of your sincere faith, a faith that dwelt first in your grandmother Lois and your mother Eunice and now, I am sure, dwells in you as well.

2 TIMOTHY 1:5 ESV

Everyone who has been fathered by God does not practice sin, because God's seed resides in him, and thus he is not able to sin, because he has been fathered by God.

1 JOHN 3:9 NET

Pure and undefiled religion before God and the Father is this: to visit orphans and widows in their trouble, and to keep oneself unspotted from the world.

JAMES 1:27 NKJV

From now on you are not strangers and people who are not citizens. You are citizens together with those who belong to God. You belong in God's family.

EPHESIANS 2:19 NLV

He helps orphans and widows, and he loves foreigners and gives them food and clothes.

DEUTERONOMY 10:18

But it is no shame to suffer for being a Christian. Praise God for the privilege of being in Christ's family and being called by his wonderful name!

1 PETER 4:16 TLB

For you did not receive the spirit of slavery to fall back into fear, but you have received the Spirit of adoption as sons, by whom we cry, "Abba! Father!" The Spirit himself bears witness with our spirit that we are children of God.

ROMANS 8:15–16 ESV

PRAYER

Father, you are my heavenly Father. You have not given me a spirit of slavery that leads to fear, but you adopted me into your family.

You created me to be your child, forming me in my mother's womb. What a great love you have for me. Before I was born, you had great plans for my life. Thank you, Father, for accepting me into your family. Today, I turn away from sin and choose to serve you as my heavenly Father and follow your Son, Jesus.

I bless my own family. I forgive them for ways they did not exemplify your heart for me. Forgive me for not doing my part to have a family that honors you. Make things right in our relationships. Heal us and help us to be the family you want us to be. Amen.

Fear

The most pervasive spirit in our world today that continually seeks to attach itself to people is the spirit of fear. This world provides many opportunities for a person to lose his or her emotional balance. There are many threats to our families, finances, friends, children, and jobs, and the spirit of fear is waiting to take advantage of our fears. In addition to these factors are all the traumatic events that come into our lives that wound us and provide opportunities for the enemy to exploit.

We can learn through many examples in the Bible that God does not want His people to fear. Instead of fear, we are encouraged to stand in awe of God, trusting that He is going to work everything out for His glory and our good. Instead of submitting to the spirit of fear because of what we see with our physical eyes, we are to rise up in the power of Christ and in the authority of Jesus, displacing fear with the faith God has put deep within us. God is our refuge and our strength; He has given us power to overcome the fear that tries to torment us.

Through Christ you can overcome fear and walk in the power, authority, and courage that God has given to us. God hasn't given you a spirit of fear, but of power and love and a sound mind. Fear doesn't have to have a place in your life today.

Promises

Don't be afraid, for I am with you.
Don't be discouraged, for I am your God.
I will strengthen you and help you.
I will hold you up with my victorious right hand.

ISAIAH 41:10 NLT

God is our refuge and strength,
an ever-present help in trouble.

PSALM 46:1 NIV

For God has not given us a spirit of fear, but of
power and of love and of a sound mind.

2 TIMOTHY 1:7 NKJV

Such love has no fear, because perfect love expels all
fear. If we are afraid, it is for fear of punishment, and
this shows that we have not fully experienced his
perfect love.

1 JOHN 4:18 NLT

The LORD is my light and my salvation;
whom shall I fear?
The LORD is the stronghold of my life;
of whom shall I be afraid?

PSALM 27:1 ESV

When you lie down, you will not be afraid;
when you lie down, your sleep will be sweet.

PROVERBS 3:24 NIV

Encourage those who are afraid. Tell them, "Be strong, fear not, for your God is coming to destroy your enemies. He is coming to save you."

ISAIAH 35:4 TLB

Even though I walk through the valley
  of the shadow of death,
I fear no evil, for You are with me;
Your rod and Your staff, they comfort me.

PSALM 23:4 NASB

PRAYER

Father God, forgive me for all the ways I have given into fear in my life. You have not given me a spirit of fear, but power, love, and a sound mind. You are my refuge and strength, and you are always with me when I find myself in trouble.

Because your presence is with me, God, I will not fear when I walk through hard times. You comfort me in the midst of the valley of the shadow of death. Jesus, because I am in you, I have no fear, for perfect love casts out all fear in my life. Give me a fearless heart—your heart—in Jesus' name I pray, amen.

Finances

The creativity and imagination God gave to humans has inspired millions of goods to become useful for daily activities, communication, travel, and income. God truly gives us the ability to gain wealth in order to take care of our personal needs as well as to help others and finance the gospel.

Wealth is not to be hoarded and buried. It is to be used to further His work on the earth. Wealth requires work, wisdom, and more work and more wisdom over a lifetime. If you are struggling right now with your finances, God is the source of everything in your life. If He provided Jesus Christ for you—who is the greatest gift He could ever give—He will also richly provide you with all things you will need in this life.

Promises

And my God will meet all your needs according to the riches of his glory in Christ Jesus.

PHILIPPIANS 4:19 NIV

Therefore do not be anxious, saying, "What shall we eat?" or "What shall we drink?" or "What shall we wear?" For the Gentiles seek after all these things, and your heavenly Father knows that you need them all. But seek first the kingdom of God and his righteousness, and all these things will be added to you.

MATTHEW 6:31–33 ESV

Wealth from get-rich-quick schemes
  quickly disappears;
wealth from hard work grows over time.

PROVERBS 13:11 NLT

The point is this: the one who sows sparingly will also reap sparingly, and the one who sows bountifully will also reap bountifully. Each of you must give as you have made up your mind, not reluctantly or under compulsion, for God loves a cheerful giver. And God is able to provide you with every blessing in abundance, so that by always having enough of everything, you may share abundantly in every good work.

2 CORINTHIANS 9:6–8 NRSV

Honor the LORD with your wealth
and with the firstfruits of all your produce;
then your barns will be filled with plenty,
and your vats will be bursting with wine.

PROVERBS 3:9–10 ESV

PRAYER

Father, you are my source for all things. I pray that as I honor you with my wealth and with the firstfruits of all my increase, that you would cause my barns to be filled with plenty and overflow with abundance.

Father, I want to help others and give toward your work. Give me a generous heart and break any poverty mind-set off my thinking. Help me to see finances the way you and be a good steward of what you have placed in my care.

I thank you that you are able to provide me with every blessing in abundance, so that by always having enough of everything, I may share abundantly in every good work. Show me what I need to do to provide for my family and myself. Give me your wisdom to handle my resources well. In Jesus' name I ask you to bless me. Amen.

Forgiveness

Sin is an act against God's will or anything that inter-feres with or damages a relationship with God. The Bible says that the price of sin is death. However, God knew before the foundation of the world that His creation could not keep all the rules and regulations He required. In His great love, He provided a way of escape, a manner of redemption through His Son, Jesus Christ. His Son paid the price for our sin by giving His life as a living sacrifice, dying a brutal death on the cross. Nothing we do can top that act of pure love. And nothing we do will ever cause God to turn His back on us if we come to Him with a humble heart and ask for His mercy and grace.

Studying the Scriptures brings great wisdom and gives us insight on how to deal with the problem of sin and its effects. The Bible says that if we confess our sins, God is faithful and just to forgive us and cleanse us from our unrighteousness. The Bible also tells us that forgiving others is essential for our well-being, and also to receive the forgiveness we need from God.

Today is the day to let forgiveness bring freedom into your life. Ask God to forgive you. Ask others to forgive you. And then forgive others. Give God your hurts and injustices and ask Him to make things right.

Promises

He is so rich in kindness and grace that he purchased our freedom with the blood of his Son and forgave our sins.

EPHESIANS 1:7 NLT

As far as the east is from the west,
So far has He removed our transgressions from us.

PSALM 103:12 NASB

And whenever you stand praying, forgive, if you have anything against anyone, so that your Father also who is in heaven may forgive you your trespasses.

MARK 11:25 ESV

For if you forgive other people when they sin against you, your heavenly Father will also forgive you.

MATTHEW 6:14 NIV

For all have sinned and fall short of the glory of God, and are justified by his grace as a gift, through the redemption that is in Christ Jesus.

ROMANS 3:23–24 ESV

Once you were dead because of your disobedience and your many sins…. All of us used to live that way, following the passionate desires and inclinations of our sinful nature. By our very nature we were subject to God's anger, just like everyone else. But God is so rich in mercy, and he loved us so much, that even though we were dead because of our sins, he gave us life when he raised Christ from the dead. (It is only by God's grace that you have been saved!)

EPHESIANS 2:1, 3–5 NLT

PRAYER

Father, you are rich in mercy, kindness, and grace. Forgive me for sinning against you and others around me. I receive the forgiveness that you provide in Jesus Christ. Cleanse me completely from my past and make me whole. Only you love me enough to make a way to escape death and give new life. Thank you for your sacrifice, Lord.

I've also held things against others and need to forgive them so I can be free. I forgive ___ for ___ and ask that you would heal me from pain this situation has caused. I release it into your care and ask you to make things right.

Thank you for your forgiveness, your love, and your redemption. As far as the east is from the west, so far have you removed my sins from me. Thank you, amen.

God gives us freedom to choose. Sometimes we choose to use our freedom to follow Jesus; other times we follow our own will, our own way, and become enslaved to the world.

We must choose carefully. Choosing to live in the ways of God will give us great freedom to experience true life in Christ. Jesus no longer wants us bound to a sinful nature or the ways of the enemy, but He wants us to experience new and profound life in Him.

God has freedom for you. Freedom from sin, addictions, hate, hurt, grief, depression, anger…whatever has you bound. The Bible says that it was for freedom that Jesus set us free.

What do you want to be free of today? You are more than a conqueror through Jesus who loves you.

Promises

Yet in all these things we are more than conquerors through Him who loved us. For I am persuaded that neither death nor life, nor angels nor principalities nor powers, nor things present nor things to come, nor height nor depth, nor any other created thing, shall be able to separate us from the love of God which is in Christ Jesus our Lord.

Romans 8:37–39 nkjv

Jesus said, "If you hold to my teaching, you are really my disciples. Then you will know the truth, and the truth will set you free."

JOHN 8:31–32 NIV

Brothers, understand what we are telling you: You can have forgiveness of your sins through Jesus. The law of Moses could not free you from your sins. But through Jesus everyone who believes is free from all sins.

ACTS 13:38–39 NCV

Therefore, there is now no condemnation for those who are in Christ Jesus, because through Christ Jesus the law of the Spirit who gives life has set you free from the law of sin and death.

ROMANS 8:1–2 NIV

He has delivered us from the power of darkness and conveyed us into the kingdom of the Son of His love.

COLOSSIANS 1:13 NKJV

Now the Lord is the Spirit, and where the Spirit of the Lord is, there is freedom.

2 CORINTHIANS 3:17 NRSV

He is so rich in kindness and grace that he purchased our freedom with the blood of his Son and forgave our sins.

EPHESIANS 1:7 NLT

Prayer

Thank you, Father, for your great wisdom in giving us the freedom to choose. Help me to choose you each day. I know that rules won't set me free from my sin, and only your sacrifice on the cross is enough.

God, I want to know the truth and be set free to experience your glorious freedom. Thank you for purchasing my freedom with your blood. I believe in you and seek to live my life according to your Word.

Forgive me for all the ways I have not trusted that you are a God of freedom. I ask that you would help me to live in the freedom that only the Spirit gives. Fill me with your Holy Spirit and help me not to be enslaved to the ways of the world any longer. I want to experience true and abundant life in you.

By your grace and with your strength I will walk in the freedom that only you can provide. In Jesus' name I pray, amen.

Grief

We all have experienced pain or loss, which has caused grief in our lives. Grief can come from many sources: the death of a loved one (including the loss of a pet), the loss of something important, separation, job loss, disasters, theft, accidents, and more. Wherever there is grief or loss there is trauma.

Grief is a natural response to loss. God wants us to grieve so we can process and heal from the loss. In the midst of grief, God draws near to those with broken hearts. God provides comfort, giving hope and peace in the midst of grief. Not only that, but the Bible promises that God will wipe away our tears, and that He will change our circumstances for the better.

God sees your loss and knows your pain. He is your comfort and your peace. Look to him so that your heart can be whole again.

Promises

Now may our Lord Jesus Christ himself and God our Father, who loved us and by his grace gave us eternal comfort and a wonderful hope, comfort you and strengthen you in every good thing you do and say.

2 THESSALONIANS 2:16–17 NLT

And those the Lord has rescued will return.
They will enter Zion with singing;
everlasting joy will crown their heads.
Gladness and joy will overtake them,
and sorrow and sighing will flee away.

ISAIAH 35:10 NIV

To all who mourn in Israel,
he will give a crown of beauty for ashes,
a joyous blessing instead of mourning,
festive praise instead of despair.
In their righteousness, they will be like great oaks
that the LORD has planted for his own glory.

ISAIAH 61:3 NLT

But you, God, see the trouble of the afflicted;
you consider their grief and take it in hand.
The victims commit themselves to you;
you are the helper of the fatherless.

PSALM 10:14 NIV

May your unfailing love be my comfort,
according to your promise to your servant.
PSALM 119:76 NIV

PRAYER

Father, I'm in pain and am experiencing grief at my losses. In this pain, I invite you to be the God of all comfort. Strengthen me. Draw near to me and give me hope. Help me walk through this grief, heal me, and in your time turn it around and fill me with your eternal joy and hope.

I break the power of any ungodly grief and command trauma and all its effects to go in Jesus' name, never to return. Jesus, heal every area of my life that has been affected negatively. Grief will not have power over me. Sorrow and sighing, flee away, and may everlasting joy and gladness overtake me.

God, everything is in your capable hands. I ask for opportunities to comfort others with the comfort I am receiving from the Lord. In Jesus' name I pray, amen.

Guidance

Our heavenly Father provides all the knowledge, wisdom, and guidance we need to live according to His Word and good plan. We have to trust in Him and listen for His voice in our day-to-day lives. He knows about the past and what is to come, and He freely shares it with His children when we seek His guidance.

All of us experience circumstances where we need to hear from God, have Him guide us in which decision is the best to make, and know that He is guiding our steps for His glory. Whether we are facing decisions about medical issues, how to raise our children, or whether or not to accept a specific job offer, we need God to guide us in those decisions. We don't serve a God who is disinterested in our lives; rather, we serve a God who wants to be actively involved in every decision we make.

No matter what decisions you have today, know that God is by your side and His guidance is priceless. He has the answers to all situations of life. Plug into His wisdom today and listen to His voice.

Promises

Trust in the LORD with all your heart,
And lean not on your own understanding;
In all your ways acknowledge Him,
And He shall direct your paths.

    PROVERBS 3:5–6 NKJV

I will instruct you and teach you in the way
  you should go;
I will counsel you with my loving eye on you.

    PSALM 32:8 NIV

The LORD directs the steps of the godly.
He delights in every detail of their lives.
Though they stumble, they will never fall,
for the LORD holds them by the hand.

    PSALM 37:23–24 NLT

Whether you turn to the right or to the left, your
ears will hear a voice behind you, saying, "This is the
way; walk in it."

    ISAIAH 30:21 NIV

The Sovereign LORD has given me his words of
wisdom, so that I know how to comfort the weary.
Morning by morning he wakens me and opens my
understanding to his will.

    ISAIAH 50:4 NLT

My son, pay attention to my wisdom;
listen carefully to my wise counsel.
Then you will show discernment,
and your lips will express what you've learned.

PROVERBS 5:1–2 NLT

PRAYER

Thank you, Father, for your guidance and wisdom in my daily life. I pray that you would direct my steps because I know that you delight in every detail of my life—not just the big decisions I will make, but in the smallest of details.

Give me an ear to hear what you are speaking to me. I trust in you with all of my heart and I acknowledge you in every detail of my life. Guide my steps and make my paths straight.

Thank you, Lord, for discernment to know the truth and act upon it wisely. Thank you for providing all the guidance I need for today. I trust you, Lord, to lead me, for I listen to your voice. Amen.

Happiness

God created happiness and He wants His people to be happy. This is not to suggest that we will never face difficulties—Jesus said that we would encounter trials in this world. Being a Christian doesn't make us immune to suffering. Rather, Jesus promises to give us the strength to endure our suffering, and not only to endure it, but to experience His joy in the midst of it. James reminds us that we can experience joy in the midst of our trials because our suffering produces patience (James 1:2–4). Even in the midst of our trials, we can be happy because God's happiness sustains us and strengthens us.

God's joy is our strength. Trusting in His love takes away the cares of the world, causing us to rest in His joy rather than be anxious about what is going on in our lives. All we have to do is ask Him for His joy.

Ask God for His joy. Even in the midst of pain or loss, He wants to give you a life characterized by joyful anticipation that God is working all things out according to His will and good pleasure.

Promises

He will yet fill your mouth with laughter
and your lips with shouts of joy.

ЈОВ 8:21 NIV

The LORD has done great things for us,
and we are filled with joy.

PSALM 126:3 NIV

I know that there is nothing better for people than
to be happy and to do good while they live.

ECCLESIASTES 3:12 NIV

I will give thanks to the LORD with my whole heart;
I will recount all of your wonderful deeds.
I will be glad and exult in you;
I will sing praise to your name, O Most High.

PSALM 9:1–2 ESV

Rejoice in the Lord always; again I will say, rejoice.

PHILIPPIANS 4:4 ESV

For the kingdom of God is not a matter of eating and
drinking but of righteousness and peace and joy in
the Holy Spirit.

ROMANS 14:17 ESV

Then he said to them, "Go your way. Eat the fat and
drink sweet wine and send portions to anyone who

has nothing ready, for this day is holy to our Lord. And do not be grieved, for the joy of the Lord is your strength."

NEHEMIAH 8:10 ESV

PRAYER

Father, I want to be happy with a joy that only you can give. When I am suffering, I will rejoice in your promises. I accept your joy and happiness today. Let my life be characterized by a joyful anticipation that you are working all things out according to your will and turning everything into good for me.

Lord, you have done great things for me. You love me and are faithful. Help me to remember the ways you have been faithful in my life, and let the remembrance of those deeds produce a delight in my heart that sustains me through times of suffering.

Fill my mouth with laugher and my lips with shouts of joy, in the name of your Son, Jesus. Amen.

God delights in our faith and loves to demonstrate His power in our lives. He loves our conscious dependency on Him and when we call out to Him in the mist of our pain, sickness, and weakness. All our earthly troubles are opportunities to receive God's love and see His power demonstrated in our lives. Only God is fully able to take any situation and turn it into good, giving us strength to overcome. We are His children and we depend on Him alone as our creator and sustainer.

Jesus continually demonstrated His power over sickness during his life and ministry. Even though Jesus now sits at the right hand of the Father, He is still the same yesterday, today, and forever. The Jesus who walked the earth two thousand years ago is the same God who is with us today through the power of the Holy Spirit, demonstrating the same miraculous power in the lives of people.

God is able to heal, He is able to strengthen, and God is able to bring health to every area of your life. No matter what health issue you are facing today, turn to God and ask Him to demonstrate His power in your life.

PROMISES

But he was pierced for our transgressions,
he was crushed for our iniquities;
the punishment that brought us peace was on him,
and by his wounds we are healed.

ISAIAH 53:5 NIV

And He said to her, "Daughter, your faith has
made you well; go in peace and be healed of your
affliction."

MARK 5:34 NASB

And he went throughout all Galilee, teaching in
their synagogues and proclaiming the gospel of
the kingdom and healing every disease and every
affliction among the people. So his fame spread
throughout all Syria, and they brought him all
the sick, those afflicted with various diseases and
pains, those oppressed by demons, epileptics, and
paralytics, and he healed them.

MATTHEW 4:23–24 ESV

Great crowds came to him, bringing the lame, the
blind, the crippled, the mute and many others, and
laid them at his feet; and he healed them. The people
were amazed when they saw the mute speaking, the
crippled made well, the lame walking and the blind
seeing. And they praised the God of Israel.

MATTHEW 15:30–31 NIV

How God anointed Jesus of Nazareth with the Holy Spirit and power, and how he went around doing good and healing all who were under the power of the devil, because God was with him.

ACTS 10:38 NIV

Bless the LORD, O my soul,
and forget not all his benefits,
who forgives all your iniquity,
who heals all your diseases.

PSALM 103:2–3 ESV

PRAYER

Lord, I thank you that you are always able and willing to heal. I treasure your words in my heart, knowing they give life and health to my physical body. Demonstrate your power through my health condition and reveal yourself to me and to others in a greater measure.

You can heal every disease. Nothing is too difficult for you. I am healed because of the wounds you endured. Father, restore me—body, mind, soul, and spirit—to your original design for a human's body. I praise you for your wonderful benefits to me—forgiveness of sins and the healing of diseases.

I declare complete healing and ongoing divine health over myself today, trusting that you are willing and able to heal. Thank you, Jesus!

Hope

Hope is a driving force that inspires us to take that next step forward. What we want rarely happens on our timetable, yet God places hopeful expectation in front of us, which causes us to know that what we are asking for will happen sometime in the future.

Maybe we are hoping that our children will grow up in the ways of the Lord, or that our physical body will be healed. Or maybe we are hoping for a job, or a better job, or a loved one to experience a breakthrough. No matter what we are hoping for, God wants that hope to fill our vision of the future.

No matter what you are facing today, know that there is hope—in this life and the next. Jesus is the one who restores our hope, giving us faithful expectation that all of His promises will be fulfilled in His time.

Promises

May the God of hope fill you with all joy and peace as you trust in him, so that you may overflow with hope by the power of the Holy Spirit.

ROMANS 15:13 NIV

He raises up the poor from the dust;
he lifts the needy from the ash heap
to make them sit with princes
and inherit a seat of honor.
For the pillars of the earth are the LORD's,
and on them he has set the world.

1 SAMUEL 2:8 ESV

The LORD is good to those whose hope is in him,
to the one who seeks him.

LAMENTATIONS 3:25 NIV

But those who hope in the LORD will renew their strength. They will soar on wings like eagles; they will run and not grow weary, they will walk and not be faint.

ISAIAH 40:31 NIV

The Lord delights in those who fear him,
who put their hope in his unfailing love.

PSALM 147:11 NKJV

And hope does not put us to shame, because God's love has been poured out into our hearts through the Holy Spirit, who has been given to us.

ROMANS 5:5 NIV

For God alone, O my soul, wait in silence, for my hope is from him.

PSALM 62:5 ESV

PRAYER

Father, my hope is in you, and in you alone. I thank you that you are good to those who hope in you, to those who seek your face. God, I seek your face today and ask you to restore hope deep within my soul.

Forgive me for believing that your promises will not come to pass. I reject discouragement, depression, lethargy, sadness, disappointment, and all trauma that would cloud my ability to see God's door of hope for me.

I pray that you, the God of all hope, would fill me with all joy and peace as I trust in you, so that I would overflow with hope by the power of the Spirit. Let hope fuel my courage, causing me to take that next step as I journey through life with you. I delight in you, Jesus. Amen.

Identity

God chose you. He wants you in His family to live with Him forever. He has claimed you, elevated you, and promoted you as one of His royal family. And He desires to work through His children—you and me—to spread His Word to the world.

Humans are born into darkness and sin. But when Jesus enters our hearts and we become part of the royal family, we move into God's marvelous light and joy, and become seated with him in the heavenly places.

Don't reject or deny who God has made you to be or what the Father wants to do for His family. Step into your destiny as His child today, knowing that you being adopted into His family makes you a son or daughter who is set apart for God's good purposes. The world or your natural heritage no longer defines who you are; rather, you are defined by the family of God and your identity in Christ Jesus.

Promises

See how very much our Father loves us, for he calls us his children, and that is what we are! But the people who belong to this world don't recognize that we are God's children because they don't know him. Dear friends, we are already God's children, but he has not yet shown us what we will be like when Christ appears. But we do know that we will be like him, for we will see him as he really is.

1 John 3:1–2 nlt

For you did not receive the spirit of slavery to fall back into fear, but you have received the Spirit of adoption as sons, by whom we cry, "Abba! Father!" The Spirit himself bears witness with our spirit that we are children of God.

Romans 8:15–16 esv

Therefore, if anyone is in Christ, he is a new creation. The old has passed away; behold, the new has come. All this is from God, who through Christ reconciled us to himself and gave us the ministry of reconciliation.

2 Corinthians 5:17–18 esv

But you are a chosen group of people. You are the King's religious leaders. You are a holy nation. You belong to God. He has done this for you so you can tell others how God has called you out of darkness into His great light.

1 PETER 2:9 NLV

Nevertheless, God's solid foundation stands firm, sealed with this inscription: "The Lord knows those who are his," and, "Everyone who confesses the name of the Lord must turn away from wickedness."

2 TIMOTHY 2:19 NIV

In a word, what I'm saying is, Grow up. You're kingdom subjects. Now live like it. Live out your God-created identity. Live generously and graciously toward others, the way God lives toward you.

MATTHEW 5:48 MSG

PRAYER

Father, thank you for your gracious gift of adopting me into the family of God. You are my Father and Jesus is my elder brother. Thank you for making me a kingdom subject, and help me to live out my God-given identity.

Forgive me for forgetting who I am in you and for rejecting myself. I declare that I will live in the identity of a son of daughter of God today. No longer will I be defined by this world or my natural family lineage; I will be defined by God's affections set upon me.

Thank you for setting your love upon me and choosing me to be a part of your family. Amen.

Justice

Whether we ever put words to it or not, all of us have a sense of justice deep down within us. When we hear of horrific things someone has done to the innocent, no one thinks that person should just be forgiven and go on with life. Something inside of us rises up and wants to see justice. We may want God's love to touch every person, even those who do horrific acts, but there is something within us that wants justice. We are people who crave justice.

The Bible presents God as a God of justice too. In fact, the desire that we have to see justice in the world comes from being made in the image of God. Jesus was a man who came to earth and demonstrated what justice looked like—He gave justice to the poor, and He made fair decisions for the exploited.

If an injustice has been done to you, then know that the desire you feel for justice was placed there by God, and He is the one who is going to have justice in the final day. God tells us not to retaliate for what has been done to us, but rather to trust Him because He promised that He would take vengeance on all our enemies. Trust in God's justice today.

Promises

He will delight in obeying the LORD.
He will not judge by appearance
nor make a decision based on hearsay.
He will give justice to the poor
and make fair decisions for the exploited.
The earth will shake at the force of his word,
and one breath from his mouth
  will destroy the wicked.
He will wear righteousness like a belt
and truth like an undergarment.

ISAIAH 11:3–5 NLT

I know that the LORD secures justice for the poor
and upholds the cause of the needy.

PSALM 140:12 NIV

Righteousness and justice
  are the foundation of Your throne;
Mercy and truth go before Your face.

PSALM 89:14 NKJV

Beloved, do not avenge yourselves, but rather give
place to wrath; for it is written, "Vengeance is Mine, I
will repay," says the Lord.

ROMANS 12:19 NKJV

Learn to do good;
seek justice,
correct oppression;
bring justice to the fatherless,
plead the widow's cause.

ISAIAH 1:17 ESV

PRAYER

Father, I thank you that you are a God of justice. You defend the poor, make fair decisions, and long to demonstrate your righteousness and justice in the earth. Help me to feel your sense of justice for specific issues I see around me today, but also help me to know that you are the one who will take vengeance on all the injustices of the world.

I release into your hands offenses, injustices, wrongdoings, and sins that have been committed against me and those I love. I trust you to make things right. You secure justice for the poor and uphold the cause of the needy.

Heal me from the wounds of injustice and empower me to do good, seek justice, correct oppression, and bring justice to the fatherless and widow. Help me to embrace the justice of God in my own life, then seek the justice of God in others' lives too. Amen.

Life

Life itself comes from God. The Bible says that He created all things, spoke everything that exists into existence, and that He keeps everything together by His continuous speaking—He holds all things together by the word of His power. It was He who planned our lives, as well as our futures. Even though our journey may not be smooth and easy at times, we must have faith that His plans are the best for us. Just as parents and teachers teach us how to handle life, God uses our experiences to guide or redirect our lives.

Through Jesus, we not only live, but we are also re-born into a new life with Him. Sometimes people describe this experience as being born again. Jesus lives within our hearts and He freely gives us His Spirit to help us. Most will explain that they feel like a new person once they accept Jesus, asking Him to cleanse them of sin and forgive them of all the wrongs they have committed. They suddenly see differently, they understand more, and their capacity to forgive and love is greatly magnified. Our relationship and belief in Jesus not only helps us through earthly life but also permits us to enjoy eternal life with Him when our time on earth is over.

Take His hand and embrace His life today.

Promises

The thief comes only to steal and kill and destroy; I have come that they may have life, and have it to the full.

JOHN 10:10 NIV

We were buried therefore with him by baptism into death, in order that, just as Christ was raised from the dead by the glory of the Father, we too might walk in newness of life.

ROMANS 6:4 ESV

Since you have been raised to new life with Christ, set your sights on the realities of heaven, where Christ sits in the place of honor at God's right hand. Think about the things of heaven, not the things of earth. For you died to this life, and your real life is hidden with Christ in God.

COLOSSIANS 3:1–3 NLT

By this we know that we abide in Him and He in us, because He has given us of His Spirit.

1 JOHN 4:13 NASB

Prayer

Father, thank you for the abundant life that is found in Christ Jesus. My old life is no more; I am a new creation in Christ. The former things have passed away, and all things have become new.

I reject all nonlife-giving thoughts that come from the enemy—thoughts of self-doubt, self-hatred, and self-harm, which lead only to destruction. Jesus, I receive your words that I say you love and accept me, which help me to walk in newness of life.

Thank you, Father, for raising me to new life in Christ, and for helping me to set my sights on the realities of eternity and heaven, where Christ sits at God's right hand. Help me to think of the things above and forsake the ways of earth. God, you sustain me and uphold me by the life-giving power of your Word. Thank you for the abundant life you've given to me. In Jesus' name I declare new and fresh life over me today. Amen.

Loneliness

What has caused you to feel alone in the past, or maybe right now? Abandonment, neglect, or indifference from others? Maybe you don't feel others understand you. Sometimes we can feel alone when surrounded with the new and different, and our earthly source of comfort, protection, and love is no longer within reach to meet our needs.

With God on your side, you are never alone, abandoned, or neglected. As one of God's chosen ones, you can accept change as a challenge, a chance to meet new friends and experience a new adventure. Everyone feels lonely at times. Jesus Himself felt both alone and forsaken as He hung on the cross. He is the one who has promised to always be near and He will never leave you.

Once you know in your heart that God is with you at all times, you may welcome quiet times away from our world's busyness when it is just you and God. In those special moments, you will hear His voice and know His heart. With God by your side, you'll never have to experience loneliness again.

Promises

The LORD himself goes before you and will be with you; he will never leave you nor forsake you. Do not be afraid; do not be discouraged.

DEUTERONOMY 31:8 NIV

Those who know your name trust in you,
for you, O LORD, do not abandon those who
  search for you.

PSALM 9:10 NLT

No, I will not abandon you as orphans—I will come to you.

JOHN 14:18 NLT

For I am sure that neither death nor life, nor angels nor rulers, nor things present nor things to come, nor powers, nor height nor depth, nor anything else in all creation, will be able to separate us from the love of God in Christ Jesus our Lord.

ROMANS 8:38–39 ESV

The LORD is near to all who call on him,
to all who call on him in truth.

PSALM 145:18 NIV

Teaching them to observe all that I have commanded you. And behold, I am with you always, to the end of the age.

Matthew 28:20 esv

Prayer

Father, even though people may neglect or abandon me and I feel lonely, I trust that you are always with me, never leaving me or forsaking me. I give you my loneliness and draw near to you. I resist the temptation to feel rejected and know that you love me and accept me. You promised to never abandon me and to never leave me as an orphan.

I ask to *feel* your nearness each day. Greet me with your presence each morning when I open my eyes. You are a friend who sticks closer than anyone on this earth. With you by my side, God, I never have to feel alone, abandoned, or neglected. I thank you that your presence is always with me. Amen.

Love

Love can be spoken of so lightly: we love a car, food, a sunset, a movie or some other earthly object or activity. Love between people is even spoken of like this—a teenager loves her boyfriend whom she has only known for a week. Sometimes our love is just loving the way someone or something makes us feel.

God's love is much different than the world's love. His love is eternal, unrelenting, and unconditional. God so loved this world that He sent Jesus to died on the cross before we even knew Him, while we were enemies of God. God demonstrates His own love for us in giving Jesus Christ on our behalf while we were stuck in sin. In spite of our disobedience, evil behaviors, and destructive activities, God still forgives us and extends His love to us.

God's love is the greatest love you can ever experience. Other's love will always come up short, but the love of God is constant, persistent, and never changing. You will never be rejected when you run to God, for He will always accept you as you are when you come to Him. Soak in His love today and receive healing from Him. His grace is magnificent will be powerful in your life.

Promises

Satisfy us in the morning with your unfailing love,
that we may sing for joy and be glad all our days.
PSALM 90:14 NIV

Three things will last forever—faith, hope, and
love—and the greatest of these is love.
1 CORINTHIANS 13:13 NLT

For you, O LORD, are good and forgiving,
abounding in steadfast love to all who call upon you.
PSALM 86:5 ESV

Know therefore that the LORD your God is God; he
is the faithful God, keeping his covenant of love to
a thousand generations of those who love him and
keep his commandments.
DEUTERONOMY 7:9 NIV

Let love and faithfulness never leave you;
bind them around your neck,
write them on the tablet of your heart.
PROVERBS 3:3 NIV

So we have come to know and to believe the love
that God has for us. God is love, and whoever abides
in love abides in God, and God abides in him.
1 JOHN 4:16 ESV

Can anything ever separate us from Christ's love? Does it mean he no longer loves us if we have trouble or calamity, or are persecuted, or hungry, or destitute, or in danger, or threatened with death? … No, despite all these things, overwhelming victory is ours through Christ, who loved us.

ROMANS 8:35, 37 NLT

PRAYER

God, I pray that you would bring a satisfaction to my soul because of the greatness of your steadfast love toward me. I ask that the satisfaction of your love will cause me to rejoice today, overcoming any love deficits I have in my life. Help me to experience your eternal, unquenchable, and unconditional love so that I can give it away to those around me.

There is nothing that separates me from your love, God, and so I stand in the abundance of your love today. Your love is so great that when I was your enemy, you sent Jesus to the cross to die for my sins. Help me to see and feel the weight of the immensity of your love for me, in Jesus' name. Amen.

Mental Illness

Mental illness generally refers to a mental disorder that causes behavior such as schizophrenia, psychosis, dementia, serious depression, bipolar disorder, and other mental conditions that disrupt and impair everyday activities.

There are many causes of mental illness, including genetic, biological, psychological, and environmental factors. Some mental illness can come from severe stress relating to mental, physical, or spiritual abuse. Some forms of psychological behavior problems are related to brain tumors or injuries. It is important to isolate the precipitating cause if possible.

But no matter the cause of the mental illness, Jesus is able to heal *any type* of sickness and disease—even the disease of mental illness. Fix your mind upon Him today and find His perfect peace.

PROMISES

You will keep in perfect peace
all who trust in you,
all whose thoughts are fixed on you!
ISAIAH 26:3 NLT

Do not be anxious about anything, but in every situation, by prayer and petition, with thanksgiving, present your requests to God. And the peace of God, which transcends all understanding, will guard your hearts and your minds in Christ Jesus.

PHILIPPIANS 4:6–7 NIV

And do not be conformed to this world, but be transformed by the renewing of your mind, so that you may prove what the will of God is, that which is good and acceptable and perfect.

ROMANS 12:2 NASB

For God hath not given us the spirit of fear; but of power, and of love, and of a sound mind.

2 TIMOTHY 1:7 KJV

Peace I leave with you; my peace I give to you. Not as the world gives do I give to you. Let not your hearts be troubled, neither let them be afraid.

JOHN 14:27 ESV

Finally, brothers and sisters, whatever is true, whatever is noble, whatever is right, whatever is pure, whatever is lovely, whatever is admirable—if anything is excellent or praiseworthy—think about such things.

PHILIPPIANS 4:8 NIV

News about him spread as far as Syria, and people soon began bringing to him all who were sick. And whatever their sickness or disease, or if they were demon possessed or epileptic or paralyzed--he healed them all.

PRAYER

Father, thank you that you care about mental illness. Jesus, you healed *all manner* of sicknesses and diseases. I pray that you would come with breakthrough for mental illness, and you would reveal the root cause and how to deal with it so more people may be healed.

Jesus, I come to you to heal the results of any accident or injury that has caused mental illness. In Jesus' name I command the production of proper chemicals in normal amounts in my body. I curse any prions and command them to be dissolved. I also command the electrical and magnetic frequencies in my body to be in harmony and balance, and my brain and all nerves to function as you designed a human body to operate.

Father, I fix my thoughts upon you—all that is true, noble, right, pure, lovely, admirable, excellent, and praiseworthy. Help me to manage my stress well, and cause my mind to be healthy and whole, having the mind of Christ, so that I think your thoughts. I pray for total healing for my total body—mind, body, and spirit. In Jesus' name I pray, amen.

Nourishment

During certain seasons of our life, we pour out so much that we get depleted. We could be believing with friends for the restoration of their marriage or for physical health; or we could be pouring out while believing God for our own promises and those of our family. Fighting the fight of faith takes its toll on us, causing us to feel like we come to a place where we can't go any further. And it is true that we can't go any further. But that is when we need to rely upon the Lord to sustain us and nourish us.

God has promised to supply all of our needs according to His riches in Christ Jesus. This means that when we feel depleted and completely empty, like we can't make it through another day, we can trust God to nourish us and sustain us in that place. In fact, the Bible says that we will be a happy people when we nourish ourselves on the Scriptures.

If you are feeling weak or weary today, turn to the Lord, open up the Scriptures, and begin to feed yourself. God will nourish you as you engage the trials of life with a deep dependence on His presence.

Promises

And my God shall supply all your need according to His riches in glory by Christ Jesus.

PHILIPPIANS 4:19 NKJV

Happy are those
who do not follow the advice of the wicked,
or take the path that sinners tread,
or sit in the seat of scoffers;
but their delight is in the law of the LORD,
and on his law they meditate day and night.
They are like trees
planted by streams of water,
which yield their fruit in its season,
and their leaves do not wither.
In all that they do, they prosper.

PSALM 1:1–3 NRSV

Then Jesus explained: "My nourishment comes from doing the will of God, who sent me, and from finishing his work."

JOHN 4:34 NLT

Come to me, all you who are weary and burdened, and I will give you rest. Take my yoke upon you and learn from me, for I am gentle and humble in heart, and you will find rest for your souls.

MATTHEW 11:28–29 NIV

Those who sow in tears
shall reap with shouts of joy!
PSALM 126:5 ESV

So humble yourselves under the mighty power of
God, and at the right time he will lift you up in honor.
1 PETER 5:6 NLT

PRAYER

Lord, I thank you that you sustain me and nourish
me. I'm tired, Lord; I'm weary and I need to feel your
strength in my spirit. I often feel depleted from pouring
so much out for the needs of others, and even for contending for my own needs. I come to you today and eat
of your Word; feed me with the words of life.

I receive fresh strength from you today. I delight in
your Word, allowing you to give life to my roots. Nourish my soul so I can do your will. Thank you for your rest
as I take your yoke upon me. Because of you, I am like a
tree planted by rivers of living water. My leaves will not
wither and whatever I do will prosper for your glory.
Amen.

Praise

It's easy to praise God for the good things He has given to us or the successful way our life is going. We have no trouble praising Him during the times when everything is good—when our bank accounts are full, our health is great, and our relationship with Him is strong. However, God deserves to be praised even in the midst of the storms of life because God reigns whether or not the reality of our lives show it.

Today God is exercising His power all over the world and we can respond to His power and beauty by spending time praising Him. Do your circumstances look favorable, or are you contending for a breakthrough? No matter what, praise the greatness of God in *that* place. Don't let your circumstances dictate your praise. Rather, praise the greatness of God in the midst of your circumstances. Praise the Lord today—pour out praise from your heart and mouth—and you will be blessed as a result.

Promises

Why are you cast down, O my soul?
And why are you disquieted within me?
Hope in God, for I shall yet praise Him
For the help of His countenance.
PSALM 42:5 NKJV

Therefore by Him let us continually offer the sacrifice
of praise to God, that is, the fruit of our lips, giving
thanks to His name.
HEBREWS 13:15 NKJV

Bless the Lord, O my soul,
    and all that is within me,
    bless his holy name!
Bless the Lord, O my soul,
    and forget not all his benefits,
who forgives all your iniquity,
    who heals all your diseases,
who redeems your life from the pit,
    who crowns you with steadfast love and mercy,
who satisfies you with good
    so that your youth is renewed like the eagle's.
PSALM 103:1–5 ESV

I will extol the Lord at all times;
    his praise will always be on my lips.
PSALM 34:1 NIV

Sing to the LORD a new song,
And His praise from the ends of the earth,
You who go down to the sea, and all that is in it,
You coastlands and you inhabitants of them!

ISAIAH 42:10 NKJV

PRAYER

God, I come to you today despite the circumstances in which I find myself. I declare that you are mighty and you rule over all the earth. You are good. You are righteous. You are perfect in all of your ways. There is no one in heaven or on earth that is as great as you; your beauty astounds me. Thank you for your love, your provision, your kindness, your gentleness.

Give me a heart to praise you during every season of my life—the good and the difficult. Put your new song within me so that I continually offer up a sacrifice of praise. Thank you for all you have done for me and will continue to do. I give all my praise to you. Amen.

Prayer

Pain, sickness, and tragedy in this life can shut down our desire to talk God. Possibly we blame Him for what's happened, or we call out to Him and don't feel He's answered us. Or maybe we don't consider that God is personal and really wants us to talk with Him and share what's in our hearts.

Prayer simply means to communicate with God. Since God is everywhere and has promised to never leave us or forsake us, we can talk to God anytime and anywhere about anything, just as we would talk to a best friend.

Long prayers aren't necessary in order for God to hear or answer what we request of Him. Sometimes the simple prayer of "help" is the only thing that can be uttered in the time of crisis. God understands the unspoken words behind that simple cry for help—He knows the longings and intentions of your heart.

Whether you are seeking wisdom, requesting a miracle, asking Him for something specific, or just sharing what's on your mind, talk to God regularly. That's prayer. The Bible tells us that God hears us when we call to Him and He will answer.

Promises

Ask and it will be given to you; seek and you will find; knock and the door will be opened to you. For everyone who asks receives; the one who seeks finds; and to the one who knocks, the door will be opened.

MATTHEW 7:7–8 NIV

My voice You shall hear in the morning, O LORD;
In the morning I will direct it to You,
And I will look up.

PSALM 5:3 NKJV

Therefore confess your sins to each other and pray for each other so that you may be healed. The prayer of a righteous person is powerful and effective.

JAMES 5:16 NIV

Don't worry about anything; instead, pray about everything. Tell God what you need, and thank him for all he has done.

PHILIPPIANS 4:6 NLT

In the same way the Spirit also helps our weakness; for we do not know how to pray as we should, but the Spirit Himself intercedes for us with groanings too deep for words.

ROMANS 8:26 NASB

You, God, are my God,
earnestly I seek you;
I thirst for you,
my whole being longs for you,
in a dry and parched land
where there is no water.

PSALM 63:1 NIV

And this is the confidence that we have toward him,
that if we ask anything according to his will he hears
us. And if we know that he hears us in whatever we
ask, we know that we have the requests that we
have asked of him.

1 JOHN 5:14–15 ESV

PRAYER

God, I can talk to you at any time. You know my heart
and hear every word from my mouth, whether spoken
silently or proclaimed loudly. Teach me what it means
to ask, seek, and knock—to not give up on prayer until
I receive what I desire from you.

I direct my voice to you in the morning and talk to
you as I go to bed each night. I want our relationship to
grow and deepen. Touch me. Heal me. Make me whole.
Lead me to pray your desires so that your kingdom
comes and your will is done on earth as it is in heaven.
Amen!

Provision

God provides. He provided for our sins to be forgiven in Christ. He provided for us to experience emotional, physical, and spiritual health. He provided the Holy Spirit so we can receive direction, comfort, and empowerment to follow Jesus and live a godly life. God provides food, water, shelter, friendship, strength, breath, and even life itself. The truth is whatever we need in life, we can come boldly to God and ask for Him to meet our needs.

Are you physically sick? Then come to God today and ask Him to heal your body. Are you in need of some sort of emotional healing or freedom from an addiction? Then come to the Lord today, for He freely gives His grace to all who ask for it. Are you in need of forgiveness of your sins? Come to God today through the blood of Jesus Christ, asking Him to cleanse you and restore you to right standing with Him. God provides us with Jesus Christ, so how will He hold back anything less than that?

Promises

If any of you lacks wisdom, you should ask God, who gives generously to all without finding fault, and it will be given to you.

JAMES 1:5 NIV

Honor the LORD with your wealth
and with the firstfruits of all your produce;
then your barns will be filled with plenty,
and your vats will be bursting with wine.

PROVERBS 3:9–10 ESV

The point is this: the one who sows sparingly will also reap sparingly, and the one who sows bountifully will also reap bountifully. Each of you must give as you have made up your mind, not reluctantly or under compulsion, for God loves a cheerful giver. And God is able to provide you with every blessing in abundance, so that by always having enough of everything, you may share abundantly in every good work.

2 CORINTHIANS 9:6–8 NRSV

And my God will meet all your needs according to the riches of his glory in Christ Jesus.

PHILIPPIANS 4:19 NIV

Therefore do not be anxious, saying, "What shall we eat?" or "What shall we drink?" or "What shall we wear?" For the Gentiles seek after all these things, and your heavenly Father knows that you need them all. But seek first the kingdom of God and his righteousness, and all these things will be added to you.

MATTHEW 6:31–33 ESV

Since he did not spare even his own Son but gave him up for us all, won't he also give us everything else?

ROMANS 8:32 NLT

PRAYER

Lord, I thank you that you provide me with everything richly to enjoy. I thank you for your best gift to me—Jesus Christ—to forgive my sin and allow me to draw near to you. I want to honor you with what you have already provided for me, and be faithful with what you will provide for me in the future.

You provide me with every blessing in abundance. I will always have enough and will be able to share abundantly with others in every good work. I seek you first and thank you for meeting all my needs according to your riches in Christ Jesus. Amen.

Being perfect in God's eyes is totally impossible. No human has been able to meet God's standard through personal effort or sacrifice to gain right standing with Him. The Bible shows us generations of people who failed to change their hearts and improve their behavior. God sent prophets, judges, and kings to help them along the way, to help them see what was right and walk in the commands of God. Even though they listened at points throughout history, in general they closed their ears and hearts to what God asked of them for their own good.

God's only choice was to send Jesus to redeem all humankind from their sin. God then gave us a choice, whether or not we are going to accept what God has provided. Are we going to continue to try to live a good life and gain our purity by our own power and strength, or are we going to be truly free from the dominion of sin by trusting in the sacrifice of Jesus on the cross and the ongoing work of the Holy Spirit in our lives?

God made a way for you to be saved and have eternal life. In addition, He gave His Word and Holy Spirit to show us how to live happily, holy, and productively while on earth. Ask Jesus to purify your heart and fill you with His Holy Spirit today.

Promises

Finally, brothers, whatever is true, whatever is honorable, whatever is just, whatever is pure, whatever is lovely, whatever is commendable, if there is any excellence, if there is anything worthy of praise, think about these things.

PHILIPPIANS 4:8 ESV

Do everything without grumbling or arguing, so that you may become blameless and pure, "children of God without fault in a warped and crooked generation." Then you will shine among them like stars in the sky as you hold firmly to the word of life. And then I will be able to boast on the day of Christ that I did not run or labor in vain.

PHILIPPIANS 2:14–16 NIV

Pure and genuine religion in the sight of God the Father means caring for orphans and widows in their distress and refusing to let the world corrupt you.

JAMES 1:27 NLT

Work at living in peace with everyone, and work at living a holy life, for those who are not holy will not see the Lord.

HEBREWS 12:14 NLT

Who may climb the mountain of the LORD?
  Who may stand in his holy place?
Only those whose hands and hearts are pure,
  who do not worship idols
  and never tell lies.
They will receive the LORD's blessing
  and have a right relationship with God their savior.
Such people may seek you
  and worship in your presence, O God of Jacob.

PSALM 24:3–6 NLT

PRAYER

Father, forgive me for all the ways I have sought to make myself right with you by my good works. I recognize that it is only through you that I can ever hope to improve and be acceptable in your sight. Show me, Lord, what to do to keep my mind and heart pure. Help me to trust solely and completely in Jesus' sacrifice on the cross and what the Bible tells me to do to live a holy life.

God, give me the grace I need to follow your ways, allowing the Spirit to produce holiness in my life. Help me not to experience just an understanding of Jesus' atonement, but also to walk in the power of it, living a life of purity and holiness. God, I want my thoughts, words, and deeds to be pleasing in your sight. Purify me. Amen.

Purpose

What is your purpose in life? Only God has the real answer to this question, but for some reason He doesn't paint a picture across the sky revealing the plan for which He created us. He uses people and experiences to nurture and guide each of us down a unique, customized path.

Some learn their purpose early in life, while others spend a lifetime questioning their identity. Only through seeking God's will and cooperating with Him can we discover life's purpose and find the reason for our birth. You never know what impact your life truly can have. Perhaps the next president of a nation or doctor who will save your grandchild's life needs a kind word today—not from someone else, but from you.

If you have believed lies about your purpose or that you don't have a purpose, have faith in God to fulfill His purpose in your life, which is the reason for your birth. Your purpose may totally surprise you. Trust Him. Be a blessing right where you are. Go where He sends you. Speak and touch the person He leads you to. He trains and guides you through life toward His purpose. Follow His direction today, for He created you for great and wonderful things.

Promises

No, dear brothers and sisters, I have not achieved it, but I focus on this one thing: Forgetting the past and looking forward to what lies ahead, I press on to reach the end of the race and receive the heavenly prize for which God, through Christ Jesus, is calling us.

Philippians 3:13–14 NLT

Whatever you do, work heartily, as for the Lord and not for men.

Colossians 3:23 ESV

To every thing there is a season, and a time to every purpose under the heaven.

Ecclesiastes 3:1 KJV

And we know that all things work together for good to them that love God, to them who are the called according to his purpose.

Romans 8:28 KJV

God has now revealed to us his mysterious plan regarding Christ, a plan to fulfill his own good pleasure. And this is the plan: At the right time he will bring everything together under the authority of Christ—everything in heaven and on earth. Furthermore, because we are united with Christ, we have received an inheritance from God, for he chose us in advance, and he makes everything work out according to his plan.

PRAYER

Father, you have a divine purpose for my life—something you have created only me to do. I anticipate what you—the Creator of the universe—have planned for me. Help me to trust you and go wherever you send me to fulfill your will through my life. I resist distraction and the cares of this life that try to hinder your purpose.

I leave everything behind and press toward the goal of knowing Christ Jesus my Lord. Until that day when I fully realize your purposes in my life and the reason you created me, help me to continue doing your will, making a difference wherever I can for Jesus' sake. Amen.

Reconciliation

Negative actions and words cause division. As a result, peace is destroyed, cooperation disappears, and relationships are broken. Reconciliation is what we need to restore our relationship to God and others—to experience harmony, peace, collaboration, and partnership to fulfill God's purposes.

Repentance, forgiveness, and understanding help relationships to be reconciled. Acknowledging our own wrongs and asking for forgiveness is the first step toward reconciliation. Extending forgiveness to others who have wronged us is essential to keep relationships healthy and whole. Unforgiveness is a poison that we drink, only hoping that the other person will get sick. If we don't forgive, we are the ones who will get sick; unforgiveness opens the door to many illnesses and diseases. But in and through Christ we can be reconciled in all of our relationships, bringing health and wholeness into our lives.

God has called you to be a minister of reconciliation—to reconcile people to God and to each other. What does that practically look like for you? Today give to God the injustices and hurts you've been holding onto. Repent, forgive, and seek to see the people and situations of your life through God's eyes.

Promises

So we have stopped evaluating others from a human point of view. At one time we thought of Christ merely from a human point of view. How differently we know him now! This means that anyone who belongs to Christ has become a new person. The old life is gone; a new life has begun!

And all of this is a gift from God, who brought us back to himself through Christ. And God has given us this task of reconciling people to him. For God was in Christ, reconciling the world to himself, no longer counting people's sins against them. And he gave us this wonderful message of reconciliation. So we are Christ's ambassadors; God is making his appeal through us. We speak for Christ when we plead, "Come back to God!" For God made Christ, who never sinned, to be the offering for our sin, so that we could be made right with God through Christ.

2 Corinthians 5:16–21 NLT

Put on then, as God's chosen ones, holy and beloved, compassionate hearts, kindness, humility, meekness, and patience, bearing with one another and, if one has a complaint against another, forgiving each other; as the Lord has forgiven you, so you also must forgive.

Colossians 3:12–13 ESV

And not only that, but we also rejoice in God through our Lord Jesus Christ, through whom we have now received the reconciliation.

ROMANS 5:11 NKJV

And whenever you stand praying, forgive, if you have anything against anyone, so that your Father also who is in heaven may forgive you your trespasses.

MARK 11:25 ESV

For if you forgive other people when they sin against you, your heavenly Father will also forgive you.

MATTHEW 6:14 NIV

PRAYER

Father, thank you for reconciling me to yourself through the death and resurrection of Jesus. Restore relationships that are broken in my life. Just as you have forgiven me, help me to be quick to forgive others. I release these sins to you and ask you to make things right.

Make me a minister of reconciliation. Give me a compassionate heart filled with kindness, humility, and patience. Fill me with your Spirit to love others and call them back to you. Amen.

Relationships

People were created to have a relationship with God and relationships with one another. For those who have been born into the family of God, we are also counted as His friends. How powerful, how wonderful is that personal relationship between God and us. He is the best friend anyone can possibly have, promising to never leave us or forsake us. Our relationship with God is the most important relationship we will ever have on this earth, and it is more than worth our time to invest into it.

God also created us to have a strong, personal bond with each other—to grow together, laugh together, and play together. Classmates, neighbors, coworkers, family members—friendships develop at all levels and stages of life. True friendships surpass time, experiences, and distance.

God has good relationships for you—friends that will encourage, challenge, and refresh you. The best friend you'll ever have is Jesus, and He also will put people around you to be His hands and feet to you.

Promises

"This is my commandment, that you love one another as I have loved you. Greater love has no one than this, that someone lay down his life for his friends. You are my friends if you do what I command you. No longer do I call you servants, for the servant does not know what his master is doing; but I have called you friends, for all that I have heard from my Father I have made known to you."

JOHN 15:12–15 ESV

Love prospers when a fault is forgiven,
but dwelling on it separates close friends.

PROVERBS 17:9 NLT

To one who listens, valid criticism
is like a gold earring or other gold jewelry.
Trustworthy messengers refresh like snow in summer.
They revive the spirit of their employer.

PROVERBS 25:12–13 NLT

Two are better than one,
because they have a good return for their labor:
If either of them falls down,
one can help the other up.
But pity anyone who falls
and has no one to help them up.

ECCLESIASTES 4:9–10 NIV

Perfume and incense bring joy to the heart,
and the pleasantness of a friend
springs from their heartfelt advice.

PROVERBS 27:9 NIV

Love each other with genuine affection, and take
delight in honoring each other.

ROMANS 12:10 NLT

As iron sharpens iron,
so a friend sharpens a friend.

PROVERBS 27:17 NLT

PRAYER

Father, I'm amazed that I can be your friend. I want to be a faithful friend to you and to those you put in my life. Provide good friends to help me grow and develop into what you desire me to be. Bring across my path those you want me to befriend. Help me to have close relationships that are trustworthy.

Fill me with your love so that I can love others with genuine affection, reviving their spirits with encouraging words and thoughtful actions. I cherish the relationships you've put in my life. Amen.

Refreshment

When we come to Christ for the very first time, He takes what is old and gives us new life. He refreshes us to become alive in Him. We are able to plug into God through prayer and meditating on His Word.

If your spiritual life has become dry or stagnant, Jesus wants to breathe new life into you today, tomorrow, and every day. We are to be continually filled with the life and presence of the Holy Spirit.

Today is your day. Jesus loves you and wants to talk to you right now, right where you are. He will renew your spirit, body, and soul and help with your troubles. He knows the best way to give you peace, joy, and new life. Don't be concerned about next month or next year. Just ask Him what He wants you to do next. He will breathe refreshment into your soul, causing you to swell with new life once again.

Promises

Take my yoke upon you. Let me teach you, because I am humble and gentle at heart, and you will find rest for your souls.

MATTHEW 11:29 NLT

Do not lie to one another, seeing that you have put off the old self with its practices and have put on the new self, which is being renewed in knowledge after the image of its creator.

COLOSSIANS 3:9–10 ESV

But that is not the way you learned Christ!— assuming that you have heard about him and were taught in him, as the truth is in Jesus…and to be renewed in the spirit of your minds, and to put on the new self, created after the likeness of God in true righteousness and holiness.

EPHESIANS 4:20–21, 23–24 ESV

Jesus replied, "Anyone who drinks this water will soon become thirsty again. But those who drink the water I give will never be thirsty again. It becomes a fresh, bubbling spring within them, giving them eternal life."

JOHN 4:13–14 NLT

A generous person will prosper;
whoever refreshes others will be refreshed.

PROVERBS 11:25 NIV

On the last and greatest day of the festival, Jesus stood and said in a loud voice, "Let anyone who is thirsty come to me and drink. Whoever believes in me, as Scripture has said, rivers of living water will flow from within them."

JOHN 7:37–38 NIV

PRAYER

Father, I come to you today to experience refreshment. I'm tired and I'm weary. I need you to breathe fresh life into me. Come to me now and teach me to drink from the life-giving water you offer so freely in Christ.

I come to you and drink deeply from your Spirit. Let rivers of living water bubble up within me and flow through me. I cast aside the old and clothe myself with the attributes of Jesus today. Fill me with your Holy Spirit. Renew my mind and refresh my perspective so that I can live with strength and vitality all the days of my life. Amen.

Restoration

Often people will have a new bounce in their step after asking God to take over their lives. They stand up taller and walk with much more confidence. Even a person's facial expression looks younger. Things are new. Life has been restored. This is because God is in the business of restoration. God specializes in taking our broken lives, our broken hopes and dreams, and even our broken bodies, and bringing restoration to them, breathing new life and hope into them.

If you have given up on a promise from God, He can restore your faith and breathe hope into your heart. Maybe you have given up on God's healing power in your physical body. God can restore your body and bring healing to your soul. He can turn your mourning into dancing, take away your sadness, and clothe you with joy. God wants to restore things in your life that have been lost or stolen. Trust Him today for the restoration He longs to bring to you.

PROMISES

Turn and answer me, O Lord my God!
Restore the sparkle to my eyes, or I will die.
But I trust in your unfailing love.
I will rejoice because you have rescued me.
PSALMS 13:3, 5 NLT

He makes me lie down in green pastures;
He leads me beside quiet waters.
He restores my soul;
He guides me in the paths of righteousness
For His name's sake.

PSALM 23:2–3 NKJV

The Spirit of the Sovereign Lord is upon me,
for the Lord has anointed me
to bring good news to the poor.
He has sent me to comfort the brokenhearted
and to proclaim that captives will be released
and prisoners will be freed.
He has sent me to tell those who mourn
that the time of the Lord's favor has come,
and with it, the day of God's anger
  against their enemies.
To all who mourn in Israel,
he will give a crown of beauty for ashes,
a joyous blessing instead of mourning,
festive praise instead of despair.
In their righteousness, they will be like great oaks
that the Lord has planted for his own glory.

ISAIAH 61:1–3 NLT

"So I will restore to you the years that the swarming
locust has eaten...
You shall eat in plenty and be satisfied,
And praise the name of the Lord your God,

Who has dealt wondrously with you;
And My people shall never be put to shame.
Then you shall know that I am in the midst of Israel:
I am the Lord your God
And there is no other.
My people shall never be put to shame."

JOEL 2:25–27 NKJV

You have turned my mourning into joyful dancing.
You have taken away my clothes of mourning and
clothed me with joy.

PSALM 30:11 NLT

PRAYER

Lord, you are always faithful to your promises. Thank you for saving me and calling me to live for you, not because of what I have done, but according to your own purpose and grace. You take away my burdens and free me from strife, stress, and trauma. Restore the sparkle in my eyes. Turn my mourning into dancing, and take away my clothes of mourning and cloth me with joy. You are a God of restoration, and you love to restore everything in my life that has been lost. Restore my soul, health, relationships, and finances. I declare restoration over my life today in Jesus' name, amen.

Throughout the Bible we can see God's promises to protect His people and keep them safe. God is a refuge—a strong tower to run to in times of trouble. When we face troubles in this life, when we experience fear and are in harm's way, we can run to the Lord who protects us, keeps us safe, and preserves us for His plans and purposes.

When times get tough, where or to whom do you turn? Do you seek to make yourself feel safe by what you can do or by running to a friend to share in your struggles? Or do we turn to the Lord and ask for His protection?

In every situation you find yourself in, God wants for you to call out to Him for protection. When you are faced with trying circumstances, turn your eyes to the Lord God Almighty. He will protect you. Call out to God and He will be your protector and your shelter in times of trouble.

Promises

If you make the LORD your refuge,
if you make the Most High your shelter,
no evil will conquer you;
no plague will come near your home.
For he will order his angels
to protect you wherever you go.

> PSALM 91:9–11 NLT

But the Lord is faithful, and he will strengthen you
and protect you from the evil one.

> 2 THESSALONIANS 3:3 NIV

The LORD also will be a refuge for the oppressed,
A refuge in times of trouble.
And those who know Your name will put
   their trust in You;
For You, LORD, have not forsaken those
   who seek You.

> PSALM 9:9–10 NKJV

The name of the Lord is a strong tower;
The righteous runs into it and is safe.

> PROVERBS 18:10 NASB

O God, listen to my cry!
Hear my prayer!
From the ends of the earth,

The LORD himself goes before you and will be with you; he will never leave you nor forsake you. Do not be afraid; do not be discouraged.

DEUTERONOMY 31:8 NIV

I cry to you for help
when my heart is overwhelmed.
Lead me to the towering rock of safety,
for you are my safe refuge,
a fortress where my enemies cannot reach me.
Let me live forever in your sanctuary,
safe beneath the shelter of your wings!

PSALM 61:1–4 NLT

PRAYER

Thank you for your protection, Father. You are my safe place. I find refuge under the shadow of your wings, for you are my refuge in times of trouble. When in harm's way, I will put my trust in you, for you, Lord, have not forsaken those who seek you. You are a strong tower that I run to, for I know I will be safe in you. Thank you for posting your angels around me to guard me. I no longer have to live in fear because you are always there for me—you are always with me. Amen.

Serious diseases can be fatal to the human body, including strokes, cancers, heart disease, lung disease, and blood diseases. It seems that when a person is diagnosed with one of these illnesses, greater faith must be exhibited for healing to occur. But the faith that believes God to heal a minor fever is the same mustard seed of faith that can drive out serious illnesses. God loves to heal people. He is all powerful, able and willing to heal any disease.

There are many different diseases that attack the human body, and they have one goal in mind—death and destruction. So instead of the person only fighting the disease, he or she has to fight all of the stress, fear, and trauma that goes along with that diagnosis. Renouncing the spirit of that disease (like cancer) is necessary in order for healing to occur. Then healing prayers must be directed to total recovery of the damaged cells and organs of the body.

Regardless of what you need healing from today, believe that nothing is impossible for the person who has faith—even "incurable" diseases. The mustard seed of faith is enough to move mountains, and that is the faith that God has placed within you. Trust Him that He can move mountains on your behalf.

Promises

You shall serve the LORD your God, and he will bless your bread and your water, and I will take sickness away from among you. None shall miscarry or be barren in your land; I will fulfill the number of your days.

EXODUS 23:25–26 ESV

He forgives your sins—every one.
He heals your diseases—every one.
He redeems you from hell—saves your life!
He crowns you with love and mercy—
   a paradise crown.
He wraps you in goodness—beauty eternal.
He renews your youth—you're always young
   in his presence.

PSALM 103:3–5 MSG

Then Jesus said to the disciples, "Have faith in God. I tell you the truth, you can say to this mountain, 'May you be lifted up and thrown into the sea,' and it will happen. But you must really believe it will happen and have no doubt in your heart. I tell you, you can pray for anything, and if you believe that you've received it, it will be yours."

MARK 11:22–24 NLT

"What do you mean, 'If I can'?" Jesus asked. "Anything is possible if a person believes."

MARK 9:23 NLT

PRAYER

God, you said that anything is possible to the person who believes. You also said that if we had the faith the size of a mustard seed, we could remove mountains by speaking to them. I take the faith that you have given to me today and I decree total healing from this illness in my life. What the doctors have called "incurable" you call curable. Nothing is too hard for you to overcome, so I pray that you would work healing in my body.

I renounce the spirit of this sickness and command all fear, stress, and trauma that has come with it to go. I break it's power in Jesus' name and speak life and restoration to every damaged cell. Return all chemicals and hormones to normal. Any organs that need replacing, Father, I know you can and will restore them to normal function in Jesus' name. I place all my cares upon you because you care for me. I speak peace to my body and my mind, and thank you for healing me in Jesus' name. Amen.

Sexuality

Temptation comes in many different forms. Enticements are everywhere with few voices explaining why morality and purity are still important for our society.

Each of us answers to God for the secret things buried in our hearts. God knows what we say, what we do, and what we think. Nothing is hidden from His eyes.

If you are struggling with your sexual identity, there is healing for you in Christ, for you were created either male or female in the image of God. If you are struggling with issues of pornography, lusts, or addictions to sexual sins, then know that healing is available for you as well. You are a child who is born in the image and likeness of God, and God has given you your sexuality for a specific purpose and for His glory. No matter what type of sexual issue you are facing today, know that God cares about your struggles and your past, and He will bring deep healing into your life.

Promises

How can a young person stay on the path of purity?
By living according to your word.

PSALM 119:9 NIV

Run from sexual sin! No other sin so clearly affects
the body as this one does. For sexual immorality is
a sin against your own body. Don't you realize that
your body is the temple of the Holy Spirit, who lives
in you and was given to you by God? You do not
belong to yourself, for God bought you with a high
price. So you must honor God with your body.

1 CORINTHIANS 6:18–20 NLT

So put to death the sinful, earthly things lurking
within you. Have nothing to do with sexual
immorality, impurity, lust, and evil desires. Don't
be greedy, for a greedy person is an idolater,
worshiping the things of this world…. Put on your
new nature, and be renewed as you learn to know
your Creator and become like him.

COLOSSIANS 3:5, 10 NLT

There is therefore now no condemnation to those
who are in Christ Jesus, who do not walk according
to the flesh, but according to the Spirit. For the law
of the Spirit of life in Christ Jesus has made me free
from the law of sin and death. For what the law

could not do in that it was weak through the flesh, God did by sending His own Son in the likeness of sinful flesh, on account of sin: He condemned sin in the flesh, that the righteous requirement of the law might be fulfilled in us who do not walk according to the flesh but according to the Spirit.

ROMANS 8:1–4 NKJV

Prayer

Father, I thank you that you have made my body to be a temple of the Holy Spirit. I am no longer my own, but I belong to you because you purchased me with a great price—the blood of Jesus Christ. God, help me to honor you with my body. Show me how I am created in your divine image. I ask that you would give me the grace to run away from sexual sin and to stay on the path of purity by living according to your Word. Forgive me for all the ways I have misused my body to fulfill its sexual appetites. I turn away from those sins now. Thank you, Jesus, that your blood washes me from all sin, and that the deeds of the body are put to death because I have a new nature in you. Strengthen my identity in you, in Jesus' name, amen!

Sickness

We live in a world that is marred by sin, which means that our bodies eventually wear out and we will eventually face death. Death will come to all of us, but prior to death we experience weakness in our physical bodies, the decay that is continually working in us. Whether cancer or a cold, diabetes or a bone break, we all face some sort of sickness in our physical bodies.

The Bible says that when we are sick, we can come boldly to the throne of God, asking for grace and mercy in our time of need. Though our bodies don't feel well, God still rules over our circumstances and Jesus still has the power and authority to heal us, not to mention His willingness and ability to do so.

Approach Jesus with faith and expectancy, believing that He still heals the sick, sets us free, and exercises dominion over our physical bodies. We will all eventually die, but that doesn't mean that Jesus isn't interested in healing your body today. Confidently call out to Him to bring healing into your life.

Promises

Let us therefore come boldly to the throne of grace, that we may obtain mercy and find grace to help in time of need.

HEBREWS 4:16 NKJV

Bless the LORD, O my soul,
and all that is within me,
bless his holy name!
Bless the LORD, O my soul,
and forget not all his benefits,
who forgives all your iniquity,
who heals all your diseases.

PSALM 103:1–3 ESV

When she heard about Jesus, she came up behind him in the crowd and touched his cloak, because she thought, "If I just touch his clothes, I will be healed."

MARK 5:27–28 NIV

The centurion replied, "Lord, I do not deserve to have you come under my roof. But just say the word, and my servant will be healed." … Then Jesus said to the centurion, "Go! Let it be done just as you believed it would." And his servant was healed at that moment.

MATTHEW 8:8, 13 NIV

PRAYER

Jesus, I thank you that you have both the power and authority to heal my body. I boldly come to you today to ask for your grace and healing power to be at work in my body. I trust that you are powerful and looking for an opportunity to show your power in my body. Cause this sickness to leave my body in Jesus' name. I break the power of stress and trauma and release your peace.

I speak to every part of my body and say, "Be whole in Jesus' name." Function properly—the way God designed you to function. I command all pain to go and full mobility to be restored in Jesus' name. I command all muscles, tendons, and ligaments to go to the place God designed you to be. Be whole and strengthen in Jesus' name. Inflammation and swelling, be healed. All chemicals and hormones in my body, be in balance in Jesus' name.

Jesus, send your word and heal me today. You paid the price for my healing, so I trust that you are at work in me. Holy Spirit, fill every part of me with your supernatural presence. Drive out all that is not good, holy, and true. I receive the healing you have for me today in Jesus' name, amen.

Strength

God not only gives life, but He also gives us strength, love, protection, and freedom. He provides all things we need to live in victory in this life. As we face difficult circumstances, it's easy to get so consumed with the daily battle that we lose a sense of God's strength working in and through us.

God is the one who gives us the strength to carry on. He gives strength to the powerless, power to the weak, and rest to those who are exhausted. Putting on the full armor of God makes us strong in the Lord and in the power of His might. He alone can win the battle on our behalf; He alone can give us strength. We need to operate from the strength that comes from heaven, not strength we can muster up throughout our own willpower.

Hope in God will give you the strength to take your next step, whether for the activities of daily living or the next battle you may face. Your strength comes from the Lord.

Promises

Have you never heard?
Have you never understood?
The LORD is the everlasting God,
the Creator of all the earth.
He never grows weak or weary.
No one can measure the depths of
  his understanding.
He gives power to the weak
and strength to the powerless.
Even youths will become weak and tired,
and young men will fall in exhaustion.
But those who trust in the LORD will find
  new strength.
They will soar high on wings like eagles.
They will run and not grow weary.
They will walk and not faint.

ISAIAH 40:28–31 NLT

Finally, be strong in the Lord and in his mighty
power. Put on the full armor of God, so that you can
take your stand against the devil's schemes.

EPHESIANS 6:10–11 NIV

Both riches and honor come from You,
And You reign over all.
In Your hand is power and might;
In Your hand it is to make great

And to give strength to all.
Now therefore, our God,
We thank You
And praise Your glorious name.

1 CHRONICLES 29:12–13 NKJV

God is our refuge and strength,
A very present help in trouble.
Therefore we will not fear...

PSALM 46:1–2 NKJV

PRAYER

Father, you are the everlasting God. You never grow weak or weary. You give power to the weak and strength to the powerless. By your grace, I will be strong in the Lord and in the power of your might. Fill me with your power, Holy Spirit. Let me find new strength as I trust in you. Help me to soar on the heights like eagles—to run and not get weary, to walk and not faint. In your hand is power and might, and I receive from your hand all that I need. Give me the strength I need today to follow you and obey your Word. Amen.

Stress

Some stress is normal; other stress is unnecessary. Taking a test, for example, can be stressful, especially if you aren't prepared for it; however, that's normal and the stress is only temporary. However, being involved in an accident, receiving a report of a serious illness, or losing a job brings long-term stress that is not quickly remedied.

Another form of stress can come from physical, emotional, or mental trauma. A physical injury from an accident, abuse, or a weapon can be identified readily, but the invisible mental and emotional trauma is more difficult to uncover.

Uncontrolled stress can develop into fear and anxiety, which are meant to control and destroy. Trauma can embed itself into the mind as well as the body. Thankfully God has given us effective weapons to deal with the stress that tries to control our lives.

Reach out to others for the help you need to deal with the stress in your life. Also place your confidence in God and His provision to keep stress levels at a minimum. Putting all of your cares and concerns in His hands with faith in Him is the only way to maintain a balanced life.

Promises

But blessed is the one who trusts in the LORD,
whose confidence is in him.
They will be like a tree planted by the water
that sends out its roots by the stream.
>   JEREMIAH 17:7–8 NIV

Therefore do not be anxious about tomorrow, for
tomorrow will be anxious for itself. Sufficient for the
day is its own trouble.
>   MATTHEW 6:34 ESV

May the God who gives endurance and
encouragement give you the same attitude of mind
toward each other that Christ Jesus had.
>   ROMANS 15:5 NIV

In my trouble I cried to the LORD,
And He answered me.
>   PSALM 120:1 NASB

I have told you these things, so that in me you may
have peace. In this world you will have trouble. But
take heart! I have overcome the world.
>   JOHN 16:33 NIV

Come to me, all who labor and are heavy laden, and I
will give you rest. Take my yoke upon you, and learn

from me, for I am gentle and lowly in heart, and you will find rest for your souls. For my yoke is easy, and my burden is light.

MATTHEW 11:28–30 ESV

PRAYER

Father, your Word says that if I'm worried and stressed, then I can come to you and find rest for my soul. I take your yoke upon me today and I learn from you, receiving rest from your loving grace.

Forgive me for being stressed out and anxious, not trusting you to take care of my needs. I repent for any resentment and bitterness that I have been holding onto. I receive your cleansing and forgiveness now in Jesus' name. I trust that you will take care of me, and that long-term stress doesn't have to be a part of my life.

I command every spirit of trauma, stress, worry, anxiety, and fear that wants to influence me to go in Jesus' name. Holy Spirit, fill me with your presence right now. Come into every worrisome situation and take control. Whatever is true, noble, just, pure, lovely, and good report, I think upon these things. I receive your peace, your rest, and your grace today, in Jesus' name, amen.

Thankfulness

If we are to experience healing and breakthrough in our lives, it is important that we become thankful. God has blessed each of us and gratitude and praise are the appropriate responses to His goodness.

An important part of developing our relationship with our heavenly Father is to worship Him on a daily basis. Thanking God shows Him that we have faith in Him as our source, our deliverer, and our Savior. Praises to Him should always be on our lips, springing forth from our hearts, whether we are having a great day or a rough one, whether we are healthy or sick, weather we are happy or depressed.

Praise God for what He does for you and worship Him for who He is. By doing this, you are paving a smooth highway of communication and blessings between Him and you.

Promises

Enter his gates with thanksgiving,
and his courts with praise!
Give thanks to him; bless his name!
For the LORD is good;
his steadfast love endures forever,
and his faithfulness to all generations.

PSALM 100:4–5 ESV

Give thanks to the LORD, for he is good;
his love endures forever.

1 CHRONICLES 16:34 NIV

Through Him then, let us continually offer up a
sacrifice of praise to God, that is, the fruit of lips that
give thanks to His name.

HEBREWS 13:15 NASB

Sing to the LORD a new song,
And His praise from the ends of the earth,
You who go down to the sea, and all that is in it,
You coastlands and you inhabitants of them!

ISAIAH 42:10 NKJV

I will sing of the mercies of the Lord forever;
With my mouth will I make known Your faithfulness
to all generations.

PSALM 89:1 NKJV

Let your roots grow down into him, and let your lives be built on him. Then your faith will grow strong in the truth you were taught, and you will overflow with thankfulness.

COLOSSIANS 2:7 NLT

Let the saints be joyful in glory;
Let them sing aloud on their beds.
Let the high praises of God be in their mouth...

PSALM 149:5–6 NKJV

PRAYER

Father, I praise you and thank you for all you have done in my life. Jesus, no words are enough to thank you for what you did for me at the cross, for the blessings you have poured into my life. Today I come into your presence with thanksgiving, declaring that you are good.

Your steadfast love endures forever and your faithfulness to all generations. I pray that my faith would grow strong and that my heart would overflow with thankfulness. God, because of your great love toward me, I will sing of your mercies forever, and I will declare your faithfulness all the days of my life! Amen.

Victory

We are in a battle every day of our lives—against the flesh, sin, sickness, or other evils in this world. As followers of Jesus, we should eagerly expect and pray for victory because that is what Jesus promises to us.

The only reason we can pray for victory is because Jesus purchased for us everything we need to experience in life—forgiveness of sins, healing of the mind and body, deliverance from demonic influence, provision for our needs, and more. We don't gain victory because we are good enough, or pray enough, or read the Bible enough. We only have the victory because Jesus has won the battle; He has defeated the last enemy to be defeated, which is death. Knowing that should cause us to be thankful in the midst of the battle.

Let faith and hope arise within you because Jesus has won the victory on your behalf. Jesus Christ is the victor and He invites you to join Him in that victory.

PROMISES

Can anything ever separate us from Christ's love? Does it mean he no longer loves us if we have trouble or calamity, or are persecuted, or hungry, or destitute, or in danger, or threatened with death? … No, despite all these things, overwhelming victory is ours through Christ, who loved us.

ROMANS 8:35, 37 NLT

But thanks be to God! He gives us the victory through our Lord Jesus Christ.

1 CORINTHIANS 15:57 NIV

For everyone born of God overcomes the world. This is the victory that has overcome the world, even our faith. Who is it that overcomes the world? Only the one who believes that Jesus is the Son of God.

1 JOHN 5:4–5 NIV

Say to those with fearful hearts,
"Be strong, and do not fear,
for your God is coming to destroy your enemies.
He is coming to save you."

ISAIAH 35:4 NLT

When I am afraid, I put my trust in you.
In God, whose word I praise—

in God I trust and am not afraid.
What can mere mortals do to me?

PSALM 56:3–4 NIV

Finally, be strong in the Lord and in his mighty power. Put on the full armor of God, so that you can take your stand against the devil's schemes.

EPHESIANS 6:10–11 NIV

Little children, you are from God and have overcome them, for he who is in you is greater than he who is in the world.

1 JOHN 4:4 ESV

PRAYER

Jesus, you defeated death, hell, and the grave at Calvary. I thank you that there is nothing that can separate me from your love. Despite horrible earthly circumstances, you promise us overwhelming victory in Christ Jesus. You give me the faith that I need to overcome the effects of the world. I trust that greater is the one in me than the one who is in the world!

Jesus, you live in me by the person of the Holy Spirit, so cause me to rise up and trust that the victory you purchased on the cross is enough for me. Thanks be to God, who always leads me in triumph through my Lord Jesus Christ! Amen.

Wholeness

God has created each one of us with three distinct parts—a body, a soul, and a spirit. Since God is a Spirit, many assume that all He cares about is the spiritual world, not really caring too much about our soul or our body. But the truth is that God cares about *us*—and not just the spiritual part. God cares about *all* of us—body, soul, and spirit.

This is one of the reasons why Jesus came to bring wholeness into every area of our life. He is the one who heals our physical bodies, touches our emotions, and sets us free from the power of sin and death so we can experience new life in Him. When we say yes to Jesus, He enters into our hearts and begins to bring healing and restoration to each area of our life.

If you are in need of healing today—whether in your physical body, your emotions, or you need freedom in your spirit—then trust Jesus to continue the good work He has already begun within you. He cares about *all* of you, and not just the spiritual part of you.

Promises

The Spirit of the Sovereign LORD is upon me,
for the LORD has anointed me
to bring good news to the poor.
He has sent me to comfort the brokenhearted
and prisoners will be freed.
He has sent me to tell those who mourn
that the time of the LORD's favor has come,
and with it, the day of God's anger against
   their enemies.
To all who mourn in Israel,
he will give a crown of beauty for ashes,
a joyous blessing instead of mourning,
festive praise instead of despair.
In their righteousness, they will be like great oaks
that the LORD has planted for his own glory.

ISAIAH 61:1–3 NLT

Now to him who is able to do immeasurably
more than all we ask or imagine, according to his
power that is at work within us, to him be glory
in the church and in Christ Jesus throughout all
generations, for ever and ever! Amen.

EPHESIANS 3:20–21 NIV

Beloved, I pray that in all respects you may prosper
and be in good health, just as your soul prospers.

3 JOHN 2 NASB

Therefore, if anyone is in Christ, he is a new creation. The old has passed away; behold, the new has come.

2 CORINTHIANS 5:17 ESV

And it happened when He was in a certain city, that behold, a man who was full of leprosy saw Jesus; and he fell on his face and implored Him, saying, "Lord, if You are willing, You can make me clean." Then He put out His hand and touched him, saying, "I am willing; be cleansed." Immediately the leprosy left him.

LUKE 5:12–13 NKJV

PRAYER

God, I pray that you would help me to prosper and be in health, just as my soul prospers. I thank you that you care about *me*—my body, my soul, and my spirit. When you came to bring healing, you came to heal the whole person and you will do more than I can ask or imagine.

I pray that you would help me to see that you are interested in all of me and you want me to be whole. Remove every hindrance to wholeness. You have made me a new creation in Christ—the old has passed away and the new has come. I trust you for my wholeness in Jesus' name. Amen!

Wisdom

As God's child and a member of His royal family, we have special access to His help. By asking for God's help, you actually plug into God's wisdom. When you seek and ask Him for whatever it is you need, then you can operate with the mind of Christ, being confident that He will give you what you ask for.

Any time you need God's help for anything in your life, the Holy Spirit is available to assist you. He comforts, protects, guides, and counsels. You need God's wisdom to avoid mistakes and make the right decisions. Take a moment to ask Him for wisdom today, trusting that He will provide it for you.

PROMISES

Joyful is the person who finds wisdom,
    the one who gains understanding.
For wisdom is more profitable than silver,
    and her wages are better than gold.
Wisdom is more precious than rubies;
    nothing you desire can compare with her.
She offers you long life in her right hand,
    and riches and honor in her left.
She will guide you down delightful paths;
    all her ways are satisfying.

Wisdom is a tree of life to those who embrace her;
   happy are those who hold her tightly.
PROVERBS 3:13–18 NLT

God replied, "Because your greatest desire is to help
your people, and you haven't asked for personal
wealth and honor, and you haven't asked me to
curse your enemies, and you haven't asked for a
long life, but for wisdom and knowledge to properly
guide my people—yes, I am giving you the wisdom
and knowledge you asked for! And I am also giving
you riches, wealth, and honor such as no other king
has ever had before you! And there will never again
be so great a king in all the world!"
2 CHRONICLES 1:11–12 TLB

Turning your ear to wisdom
and applying your heart to understanding—
indeed, if you call out for insight
and cry aloud for understanding,
and if you look for it as for silver
and search for it as for hidden treasure,
then you will understand the fear of the LORD
and find the knowledge of God.
PROVERBS 2:2–5 NIV

For this reason also, since the day we heard of it, we
have not ceased to pray for you and to ask that you
may be filled with the knowledge of His will in all

spiritual wisdom and understanding, so that you will walk in a manner worthy of the Lord, to please Him in all respects, bearing fruit in every good work and increasing in the knowledge of God.

COLOSSIANS 1:9–10 NASB

If you need wisdom, ask our generous God, and he will give it to you. He will not rebuke you for asking. But when you ask him, be sure that your faith is in God alone. Do not waver, for a person with divided loyalty is as unsettled as a wave of the sea that is blown and tossed by the wind.

JAMES 1:5–6 NLT

PRAYER

Father, you are a generous God and I trust that you will supply me with the wisdom I need to make every decision today. Holy Spirit, you are my wise counselor, and you are the one who gives me everything I need in Christ Jesus. Help me walk in a manner that is worthy of you today by giving me spiritual wisdom and understanding to do your will.

Forgive me for leaning on my own understanding. I acknowledge your presence in my life and I want to do your will. I embrace your wisdom and apply my heart to understand your ways. Guide me in your paths today in Jesus' name, amen.

Worry

Worry is a person's fearful response to events that are beyond his or her control. It is true that there are many things to worry about in our day-to-day lives. We can worry about a job, finances, health, a spouse or children, and a myriad of other things. We are not immune to worry. However, God instructs us not to worry but turn to Him in prayer. As we do so, the peace of God guards our hearts and minds in Christ Jesus.

You can overcome anxiety through the power of the Holy Spirit. The key to overcoming anxiety and worry is to surrender control of every area of your life to Christ and trust Him to do a better job than you can. You simply cannot do it all. The peace of God is only a prayer away. As you turn to God in faithful prayer, you will experience freedom from the anxieties, cares, and worries that harass you. God is the God of peace and can give you freedom from your worries and cares.

Promises

If you make the LORD your refuge,
if you make the Most High your shelter,
no evil will conquer you;
no plague will come near your home.
For he will order his angels
to protect you wherever you go.
PSALM 91:9–11 NLT

Say to those with fearful hearts,
"Be strong, and do not fear,
for your God is coming to destroy your enemies.
He is coming to save you."
ISAIAH 35:4 NLT

In my trouble I cried to the LORD,
And He answered me.
PSALM 120:1 NASB

I have told you these things, so that in me you may
have peace. In this world you will have trouble. But
take heart! I have overcome the world.
JOHN 16:33 NIV

Don't worry about anything; instead, pray about
everything. Tell God what you need, and thank him
for all he has done. Then you will experience God's
peace, which exceeds anything we can understand.

His peace will guard your hearts and minds as you live in Christ Jesus.

PHILIPPIANS 4:6–7 ESV

Therefore I tell you, do not worry about your life, what you will eat or drink; or about your body, what you will wear. Is not life more than food, and the body more than clothes? Look at the birds of the air; they do not sow or reap or store away in barns, and yet your heavenly Father feeds them. Are you not much more valuable than they?

MATTHEW 6:25–26 NIV

Give all your worries and cares to God, for he cares about you.

1 PETER 5:7 NLT

PRAYER

Father, I put all my needs in your hands. I give you all of my worries because I know that you care for me and provide for me. You told me not to worry about food and clothing and my daily needs, so I trust you for everything in my life today. You are the one I look to in times of worry, so help me to trust you in all circumstances.

You have overcome the world! Thank you, Jesus, for giving me peace instead of worry, faith instead of fear, and hope instead of despair. Amen.

Healing Resources

With wisdom, understanding, and plenty of biblical support, Joan Hunter reveals powerful truths about healing and being whole, the authority of the believer, what opens doors to illness, freedom from guilt, being filled with the Holy Spirit, how to use what you've learned, and more. There is good news! God wants to heal every person. His power is limitless, His plan is great, and He will provide for everything. We simply have to accept his vision and believe.

In this inspiring and life-changing book, Joan Hunter shares her challenging testimony of how she overcame rejection and the worst betrayal imaginable. Learn how you can forgive, walk out your healing, and see God restore all that has been lost.

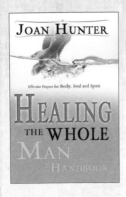

You can walk in divine health and healing. This comprehensive, easy-to-follow guidebook containing powerful healing prayers that cover everything from abuse to common infections and everything in between. This book deals with the root causes of diseases and will equip you with effective prayers for the body, soul, and spirit. By following these step-by-step instructions and claiming God's promises, you can be healed, set free, and made totally whole-body, soul, and spirit.

Contact Joan Hunter at

Joan Hunter Ministries
PO Box 111
Tomball, TX 77377-0111
Tel 1-281-789-7500
Email: info@JoanHunter.org
JoanHunter.org